being a
GREAT MOM
raising
GREAT KIDS

being a
GREAT MOM
raising
GREAT KIDS

sharon jaynes

MOODY PUBLISHERS
CHICAGO

All Scripture quotations, unless otherwise indicated, are taken from the *Holy Bible, New International Version®*. NIV®. Copyright © 1973, 1978, 1984 by International Bible Society. Used by permission of Zondervan Publishing House. All rights reserved.

Scripture quotations marked NASB are taken from the *New American Standard Bible®*, © copyright 1960, 1962, 1963, 1968, 1971, 1972, 1973, 1975, 1977. The Lockman Foundation. Used by permission.

Scripture quotations marked RSV are taken from the *Revised Standard Version* of the Bible, copyright 1946, 1952, and 1971 by the Division of Christian Education of the National Council of the Churches of Christ in the USA. Used by permission. All rights reserved.

Scripture quotations marked KJV are taken from the King James Version.

Scripture quotations marked TLB are taken from *The Living Bible* copyright ©1971. Used by permission of Tyndale House Publishers, Inc. Wheaton, Illinois 60189. All rights reserved.

All Scripture quotations marked AMPLIFIED are taken from *The Amplified Bible* ©1965 by Zondervan Publishing House; The Amplified Old Testament Part One Copyright © 1964 by Zondervan Publishing House; The Amplified Old Testament Part Two Copyright ©1962 by Zondervan Publishing House; The Amplified New Testament Copyright © 1958 by Zondervan Publishing House. All rights reserved.

The use of selected references from various versions of the Bible in this publication does not necessarily imply publisher endorsement of the versions in their entirety.

The story of the lighthouse keeper running out of oil is from *Just Like Jesus,* by Max Lucado. Copyright 1998, Word Publishing, Nashville, Tennessee. All rights reserved.

"Mama's Plan" by Marion Bond West. Reprinted with permission from *Guideposts* magazine (Sept. 1998). Copyright 1988 by Guideposts, Carmel, New York 10512.

"The Man Who Thinks He Can," author and original source unknown, is from *Victory over the Darkness,* by Neil Anderson. Copyright 1990, Regal Books, Ventura, California 93003.

Library of Congress Cataloging-in-Publication Data

Jaynes, Sharon
    Being a great mom, raising great kids / Sharon Jaynes
        p. cm.
    ISBN 0-8024-6532-3
        1. Mothers. 2. Parenting. 3. Parenting—Religous aspects—Christianity.

HQ759 .J33 2000
306.874′3—dc21

00-061663

3 5 7 9 10 8 6 4 2

Printed in the United States of America

To Steven

Being your mom has been
one of God's greatest blessings to me.
You were a great kid,
and I am so thankful
for the godly young man you have become.

Contents

Section 4: Be a Self-Esteem Builder

Section 5: Be a Seed Sower

Section 6: Be an Example Setter

Section 7: Be Diligent

$\mathcal{A}$cknowledgments

The first person to recognize and thank is my husband, Steve. If a Proverbs chapter 32 existed, it would be about him. And Proverbs 32:28–29 would read, "His children rise up and bless him, and his wife also praises him saying, 'Many men have done nobly, but you excel them all.'" His love and support have spurred me on to birth this book.

I'd also like to thank Lysa Terkeurst, my partner at The Proverbs 31 Ministry. She is my cheerleader, treasured friend, and dear sister in Christ.

I offer special thanks to my mother, Louise Edwards, for being a diligent mom. Our relationship has grown sweeter with each passing year. Thanks also to Glynnis Whitwer for reading over the manuscript and asking good questions.

I thank the staff of The Proverbs 31 Ministry for their love and support. What an awesome group of women the Lord has raised up to touch women's hearts and build godly homes. A special thanks goes to Greg Thornton and the staff at Moody Press for catching the vision of The Proverbs 31 Ministry and believing we had something to say.

Then there's my editor Janet Kobobel Grant. An excellent editor who can find?—her worth is far above rubies. Janet is a rare and wonderful gem. With a skillful pen, she marks, slashes, moves, and draws smiley faces. I appreciate her diligent commitment to excellence.

Most of all, I'm grateful to the Lord for allowing me the opportunity to encourage mothers and point them to the Savior.

CHAPTER ONE

Moms
and Blessings

*H*ave you ever noticed what happens when a television camera pans the cluster of college football players on a field's sidelines? The young men, most of whom are experiencing their first taste of national attention, call out two words. Those words make a woman's heart skip a beat, swell with pride, and melt in a puddle of love. "Hi, Mom!" the guys shout, following the greeting with wild waves and big smiles.

An inexplicable bond exists between a mother and her child. While a child is being knitted together in Mom's womb, the mother's very blood is pumped from her heart to her child's. And even though the umbilical cord is severed in the delivery room, an invisible cord holds them together for the rest of their lives. Elizabeth Stone aptly explained that bond when she said, "Making a decision to have a child—it's momentous. It is to decide forever to have your heart go walking around outside your body."[1]

And while the mother's heart is vulnerable to every pang her child experiences, that woman also realizes that God has placed another's soul in her care and given her the privilege, for a few fleeting years, to shape that soul. What will we mothers do with those years? How will we invest the time? Who can help us to know what to do?

I've often been interviewed in my role as a spokeswoman for The Proverbs 31 Ministry. Frequently I'm asked if I think the wife of noble character described in Proverbs chapter 31 is one woman or several women pooled together into a depiction of some sort of supermom. Interviewers also ask if I think the verses exemplify a typical day for Mrs. Worth More Than Rubies or a lifetime of accomplishments. I believe that she is one woman and that the listing of her achievements spans her life. Verse 28 leads me to those conclusions: "Her children rise up and call her blessed" (RSV).

I don't know about you, but I haven't heard many preschoolers bless their mothers for devoting arduous hours to potty training, for washing a favorite Mickey Mouse T-shirt, or for staying up all night cleaning throw-up. A child is more likely to rise up and call his or her mother blessed when that child is a young adult and realizes the sacrifice, hard work, undaunted love, tender affection, and wisdom that Mom has poured into his or her life for eighteen to twenty-five years. And sometimes that realization doesn't come until a child has a child of his or her own.

When I became a mother, I wondered what exactly the Proverbs 31 woman did to cause her children to rise up and bless her. To find some answers, I've observed mothers through the years, listened to what grown children have to say about their mothers and prayed that God would give me wisdom in raising my own child. *Being a Great Mom, Raising Great Kids* consists of seven mothering characteristics I've seen again and again in blessed mothers.

King Lemuel's mother, who wrote Proverbs 31, started each verse with a letter of the Hebrew alphabet to help her son remember the essential elements of a model wife and mother. In keeping with that teaching style, each of the following seven sections begins with a word formed from a letter of "B-L-E-S-S-E-D." In each section, I've included some practical ideas to help you implement the specific quality discussed and a story about a mother who expressed that quality well. And at the end of the book, you'll find fourteen Bible studies, two for each section. These studies will help you seek the Lord for ways He wishes to affirm you as a mother and for ways you could make some adjustments. You might want to gather together a group of other mothers who long to hear their children call them blessed.

My prayer for you, dear mother, is that you will not grow weary in doing good, but that this book will encourage you to keep doing what you do well and to make alterations in areas that need improvement. Most of all, I, like you, pray that one day your children will rise up and call you blessed.

SECTION ONE

Be a
Beacon

CHAPTER TWO

*A*n Immovable Landmark

*O*n February 4, 1984, my world changed forever. After twenty-three and one-half hours of blood, sweat, and tears, of heave-ho-ing, of pushing and pulling, Steven Hugh Jaynes Jr. came screaming into the world, and I became . . . a mother.

But somehow, in the bustle of leaving the hospital two days later, someone misplaced the owner's manual. After all, this was my first child, and certainly he came with instructions!

I had taken a short class at the Red Cross on child care, but I knew immediately that this experience was going to be very different from that six-week course. Steven was not made of durable plastic but of delicate skin. I couldn't leave him on the counter and come back after a fifteen-minute coffee break. And he didn't lie perfectly still while I practiced changing, feeding, and burping. He wiggled endlessly. The first time my husband, Steve, and I changed Steven's diaper, it took four hands and eleven minutes. Even then, we didn't get the tabs straight.

An eternity seems to have passed since the day we drove home from the hospital with Steven, who was lost somewhere in his oversized car seat. Now he is the one driving, and I'm the one strapped in the backseat. It has been an incredible ride! I never did locate that owner's manual, but I've discovered helps along the way. I've learned from godly women who have gone before me, from fellow travelers who are journeying down the road with me, and from my heavenly Father, who enfolds, instructs, and encourages me.

Just as God's Word has been a light to my path, I've come to realize a mother is a light to her children. I've lived in North Carolina all my life and love its sandy beaches and irregular coast. Dotting the ragged shoreline stand seven stately beacons of light. The majestic, sweeping lanterns light the way at Bald Head Island, Ocracoke Island, Cape Lookout, Bodie Island, Currituck Beach, Oak Island, and Cape Hatteras. These sentinels' distinctive designs of black-and-white diamonds, stripes, or checks tower skyward some two hundred feet, serving as landmarks for navigation. To the mariner, the lighthouse is a symbol of integrity, constancy, reliability, and aid.

Constancy

A mother whose children rise up and call her blessed is much like a stately lighthouse. She has a solid foundation in Jesus Christ. Her walls of faith are constructed to withstand the storms of life, and her primary function is to house the light of Christ. This mother is an immovable constant in her child's life, a landmark along life's journey, and a guiding light that points her child to the safe harbor of home and eventually out to sea.

Mothers used to look like my Grandma Edwards. As a child, I was sure she always had been old. She wore funny, baggy underpants and an unattractive undershirt to match, styled her gray hair in a long braid that wound around her head like a crown, and loved to watch Perry Mason, eat peanut butter crackers, and drink Coca-Cola from a chilled glass bottle. She never drove a car or frequented a shopping mall but spent her days gardening, canning, and sewing.

Mothers and grandmothers no longer spend their days like my Grandma Edwards. They are on the go, with schedules that would make the best air traffic controller's head spin. But they remain the still-point in their family's vortex of activity, the landmark each family member always returns home to.

Recently I attended a barbecue dinner with five hundred tourists in the Rocky Mountains. Across from me sat a family of four from Birmingham, Alabama: a dad, mom, and two little girls, ages eight and ten. We all introduced ourselves and began the friendly banter of "Do you know so-and-so?" and "What do you do?"

At one point in the conversation, someone asked Mary what she "did." With downcast eyes, she shrugged and said, "Oh, I'm just a mom. I don't have a job."

Immediately the hair bristled on the back of my neck, and sirens and lights went off in my head. "Just" a mom? I assured Mary that she had the most important job in all creation: to create order out of chaos; to ensure the physical, emotional, and spiritual well-being of her two little girls; to bring continuity to her family in a fast-changing world; and to shape the individuals who would contribute to our future as a community and a nation.

I think Mary was sitting up just a little straighter by the time we finished our conversation, and I don't think she'll ever use the words "just" and "mom" in the same sentence again.

Mary didn't know it, but if she hadn't responded to my initial tirade on motherhood, I was ready to launch my second missile, which was to unpack that little word "mom." What exactly is a mom's job description? She's a wife, mother, friend, housekeeper, interior decorator, laundress, gourmet chef, short-order cook, chauffeur, painter, wallpaper hanger, seamstress, nurse, guidance counselor, internal affairs CEO, financial planner, travel agent, administrative assistant, disciplinarian, preacher, teacher, tutor, spiritual adviser, dietician, lecturer, librarian, fashion coordinator, private investigator, cheerleader, manicurist, pedicurist, landscaper, hair stylist, psychologist, plumber, computer programmer, automobile maintenance expert, referee, and gift purchasing agent for both sides of the family. She might not receive a salary, but the fringe benefits are invaluable: hugs, kisses, and buckets of love. And, she hopes, one day her child will call her blessed.

Even though moms change hats from one minute to the next, we can assure our children that our love never changes, our support never tires, and our commitment to being a beacon remains unmoved. In that way, we're still like my Grandma Edwards.

Guiding Light

Not only is the mom a constant, but she also is a guiding light to her children. To fulfill that role, she must be present, available, and approachable. Sometimes this involves sacrifice. My neighbor Patty faced the realization that she wasn't being the guiding light in her children's life, and she had the courage to make a change.

While I was twenty-eight and learning to do cross-stitch, Patty was doing a little cross-stitch of her own as one of our city's most sought-after emergency room surgeons. I heard a doctor once say, "If I woke up in an emergency room and saw Patty Thomas's face and busy hands working over me, I'd just go back to sleep and rest assured that I was in the best hands possible."

Patty and her husband had their first and second sons while she was doing her residency in medical school. Her third and fourth children came along when she was working full-time in Charlotte's busiest hospital. But something happened to Patty as her first two children went off to elementary school. The Lord started doing a little heart surgery of His own.

Patty's first child was entering second grade, and she realized that she didn't know him very well. She had missed some of his milestones such as first words and first steps. Actually, this little boy knew his grandmother better than he did his mother. And as her fifth child began to kick inside her tummy, she decided that she never wanted to be a "stranger" to her children again.

So Patty made a change. She quit her job. She put away her surgical tools and began to master Lego castles, puzzles, and science experiments. She memorized state capitals, reviewed her ABCs, and gazed into her children's eyes. She took the torch from her mother and became the guiding light in her children's lives.

Now Patty is doing more than sewing people back together in a sterile operating room. She is knitting hearts, bandaging skinned knees, and kissing away tears. She is shaping and molding the now seven Thomas children to become a generation who love the Lord and influence the world for Christ.

Patty is working on her Ph.D. in motherhood. Like all other residency programs, the hours are long, the pay is low, but the rewards are immeasurable. If you asked Patty what she gave up, she would say, "Very little." Being a doctor can't compare to the joy she receives being the primary influence on her children and being the guiding light that leads them down the path of life.

Not every mother can quit her job and stay at home with her children. That doesn't mean a mother who works outside the home is an inferior or inadequate mom. But it does mean she has to be even more masterful and intentional in how she uses the time with her children. The personal sacrifices she has to make are great.

Of course, every mother is a working mother. Can we be overqualified for the job? Overtrained? Is our talent ever wasted? I don't think so.

When I was asked to speak to a group of high school girls about motherhood as a career choice, one of them asked me, "If I'm going to just be a mother one day, why do I even need to go to college?" I assured her that no amount of education or training would ever be wasted in this job. Besides, she needed not look at the job as being "just a mother" but, as one woman said, as "socializing homo sapiens into the dominant values of the Judeo-Christian tradition in order that they might be instruments for the transformation of the social order into the kinds of eschatological utopia that God willed from the beginning of creation."[1]

In light of that answer, the high school student responded, "Oh."

A mother draws on every ounce of life experience: academic, relational, and spiritual. No matter what her educational achievements, social position, or financial status, no other accomplishment is greater than to have children who one day rise up and call her blessed.

President Theodore Roosevelt said it this way:

> No other success in life—not being President, or being wealthy, or going to college, or writing a book, or anything else—comes up to the success of the man or woman who can feel that they have done their duty and that their children and grandchildren rise up and call them blessed.[2]

I believe the home is the place of greatest ministry. And no position is greater than that of a mother who is a beacon, guiding and thus protecting those who are in her home.

The mother who provides a guiding light to her children is much like the good shepherd in Scripture. Jesus tells us the difference between a good shepherd and a hired hand in John 10.

I am the good shepherd. The good shepherd lays down his life for the sheep. The hired hand is not the shepherd who owns the sheep. So when he sees the wolf coming, he abandons the sheep and runs away. Then the wolf attacks the flock and scatters it. The man runs away because he is a hired hand . . . (verses 11–13)

The shepherd is willing to lay down his life for the sheep. But the hired hand runs away because caring for them is only his job. We can't expect a day-care worker, preschool teacher, or baby-sitter to care for our children as lovingly as we do. That's not to say that we're never to utilize the help of others, but we do need to recognize the limitations of their hearts.

Four hundred years before Christ's birth, Socrates wrote, "Could I climb the highest place in Athens, I would lift up my voice and proclaim, 'Fellow citizens, why do you turn and scrape every stone to gather wealth, and take so little care of your children to whom you must one day relinquish all?'"[3] Why indeed? When we invest time in our children today, we reap the dividends for the rest of our lives.

A Landmark

I'm considered "directionally impaired." In other words, I get lost in my own neighborhood. I do fine with "turn left" or "turn right," but I can't handle "go east" or "go west." Once I do finally reach my destination, I break out in a cold sweat as I anticipate following those same directions in reverse to go back home. For me, just forget the map, don't tell me east or west, simply tell me some major landmarks along the way.

A mother who is a beacon to her children is like a landmark on life's journey. If a child becomes lost, he knows he can search for the landmark to show him the way home. If he searches but can't find his landmark, his wanderings can have devastating results.

My friend Mary told me about the emptiness she felt as a child because her landmark was often missing. She recounted an awards ceremony she attended when she was in the eleventh grade. The memory was so vivid that, even after twenty-five years, she could recall what she was wearing: "lavender bell bottom hip huggers, bubble knit short sleeve top, Dr. Scholl's wooden sandals, and a blue bandanna tied around my head of long stringy hair." This was accepted attire for teens in the seventies, except for days when a special awards or recognition assembly was held.

As Mary sat in homeroom that day, the principal announced over the intercom that an unscheduled assembly would take place at eleven that morning to recognize students inducted into the National Honor Society. That's when she understood why so many of her friends were dressed a notch above the norm. Their parents had received the traditional warning call the night before and had made sure their kids had washed their hair and the frayed jeans had stayed in the drawer.

Four hundred teens found seats in the darkened auditorium. The principal made a speech of commendation from the podium. "We are here to recognize those students who have achieved academic excellence, upheld high moral principles, and represented our school positively in the community. Will the following students come forward when your name is called to receive a certificate and a candle to be lit by last year's inductees?"

Mrs. Smith called each name, and Mary watched several of her friends walk across the immense stage. Then, to her mingled horror and delight, she heard *her* name. Delight at the honor. Horror at her shabby appearance. She thought, *Why hadn't my parents warned me?*

Standing as a weed among flowers on the stage, she panned the back of the room where proud parents snapped pictures and pointed out their progeny to others standing on tiptoe to catch a glimpse. Even though Mary held a candle in her hand, the light in her heart went dim as she realized her parents were not there . . . again.

Later she discovered that her dad had received the call from school the night before, the call that would have made most parents explode with excitement and pride. But he forgot and forgot to tell her mother. Even though they both worked just blocks from the school, they were not there . . . again. Just a few steps would have made a world of difference to one young girl who needed a landmark in her life. Far more than a candle and a piece of paper, she desired their approval. But their continued absence echoed to her that she was unimportant and held little value in their eyes.

"Going to my older brother's athletic events had been a weekly family outing," she remembered as she concluded her story to me. "But for the six years I was a cheerleader, my parents never came to a game to watch me perform. After all, he was a boy, and, well, I was just . . . I wasn't sure what I was. But I knew I wasn't important. At school plays, field trips, and class parties, the other moms took the pictures that fill my scrapbooks."

Don't think this is a bitter woman, for she isn't. Mary came to know Christ as her Savior and has found value in who she is in Him. Still, the pain of a parent's absence, the pain of lack of interest in a child's activities and accomplishments, can leave scars that last a lifetime.

As a mother, be available to your children. Be a Beacon. Be a landmark. Is there a school play? Be there. Is there a track meet where you have to sit three hours to see your child run a fifty-eight-second race? Be there. Is there an awards assembly in which your child walks across the stage to receive a ribbon, a plaque, a trophy? Be there.

No, you won't be able to go to every event, especially if you work. But imagine how your child's face will light up when you announce you've made arrangements to take off work to be there.

In an article in *Better Homes and Gardens,* Martha Miller wrote of a study interviewing forty-seven juniors and seniors in Atlanta, San Diego, and Kansas City, Missouri, who were described by their teachers as "good kids."[4] They weren't necessarily the smartest or the most popular, but these kids made good grades, emerged as leaders among their peers, and had the drive to succeed. Most were involved in sports, extracurricular activities, or had part-time jobs. Forty-six of the forty-seven planned to attend college.

Based on interviews with these students, Ms. Miller developed six parenting strategies to set children on the road to experiencing successful teenage years. Not surprisingly, the number one strategy was to *be available.* She reported that the teens said the number one encouraging factor was their parents' coming to their games.

One teen, Lisa, from Atlanta, said, "I always look up in the stands, and my dad will be there in his suit and tie. I once overheard my uncle say that my dad missed two big meetings to drive to another town to watch me in a game that I didn't even play half of. He never told me." Lisa felt valuable.

Compare that to Thomas's friend. "There's a guy on my team that's really good. My mom cut out an article in the paper about him and gave it to him to take home. He said, 'No, thanks. My mom would just throw it away.'" Undoubtedly this teen felt unimportant to his mother, and Thomas realized how special his own mother was.

Not only does attending sporting events show a child that he is valued, but it also serves as a springboard for conversation and listening, which we'll discuss in section two. "For a child, absence does not make the heart grow fonder," wrote author Brenda Hunter. "Instead, absence generates profound feelings of rejection and a yearning for love that can dominate the whole life."[5]

The time we spend with our children will be one of the best investments we will ever make. We won't be able to attend every event, but our kids need to know they are a priority to us. And keep in mind, in this mission called "parenting," it's better to build children than to repair adults.

On Guard

The beacon is a landmark that her children can always count on. She is watching out over the sea of faces to protect her tiny fleet. The Proverbs 31 woman "watches over the affairs of her household." She is present. She is available. And she is on guard.

The phrase "watch over" means "to hedge about as with thorns," much as a mother bird might protect her young with the thorny rim of a nest. These same words are also used in the Bible as a military term, such as to watch over a city.[6] Can't you just see it now—the lighthouse standing tall, not tossed by the surf but firmly grounded, guiding her children safely to shore? This beacon watches out for more than the physical safety of her fleet. She watches out for their spiritual and emotional needs as well.

Her gaze is not a casual glance. She doesn't just give her children a once-over before they rush out the door, to make sure their hair is combed and their socks match. This is a mother who actively guards, protects, saves, guides, and attends to those precious to her.

When children approach adolescence, they desire Mom to be less visible. However, they want to know the sentinel is still available. Being available for that teen after school is paramount. Teenagers need a refuge, a safe harbor after a day of social combat.

Who will they turn to? Whoever is available and willing to listen. If it isn't you, it will be someone else. And just who that someone could be is a scary thought. The time of greatest sexual activity among teens is between 3:00 and 5:00 P.M., and this sexual involvement occurs not in a car's backseat but in the teen's home while the parents are at work.

Being physically present isn't the mother's primary goal. Having the greatest impact on her home is. You can be physically present and still not have a positive impact. You can be there but not be all there. Sometimes a mother is so wrapped up in other pursuits, so focused on relational struggles, so preoccupied with keeping the castle clean and checking items off her "to do" list, so engrossed in television or a good book, that she is oblivious to the teenager who has become withdrawn and sullen or to the chubby fingers tugging at her skirt. If you're going to be there, be all there—mind, body, and soul.

Seeing Them Off

Being a landmark doesn't end when a child goes off to college. The farther a ship moves out to sea, the more important the landmark becomes. One day in a Sunday school class I attend, 150 parents of teenagers sat with an air of foreboding filling the room. Just the day before, many of these parents had seen their children off. This was the Sunday after several students had made their exodus to that wild, frenzied world of academia, experimentation, and freedom. These parents' kids had gone off to college.

Grown men were weepy, sharing their battle wounds from dropping off their baby girls at tiny, stark dorm rooms. Moms were crying unashamedly, and many were speechless for the first time in their lives.

Nancy and Bill Hall were there that day. Their son, Jordan, a sophomore, was visiting our class and witnessed these blubbering parents. In an attempt to encourage everyone, our teacher asked, "Jordan, since you haven't gone back to school yet and already have one year under your belt, can you share some words of wisdom with the class about what you feel your parents did right during your first year of college?"

With that, Jordan rose, faced the class, and replied, "I'd like to take this time to publicly thank my parents for the strong moral upbringing they gave me. I want to thank them for the way they gave me my freedom when I went off to college. But more importantly, for the way they let me come back home. They always were available when I needed someone to talk to, and they've left the lines of communication open. They've been great parents, and I'd like to publicly thank them for all they've done."

When Jordan sat down, everyone was crying, even those who didn't have children leaving for college. He had risen and called his parents blessed. His mother was a beacon, a faithful landmark who kept her light shining, welcoming him home but directing the way so he could sail out to new horizons.

Our children's growing-up years go by so quickly, and we can never turn back the clock.

My hands were busy through the day.
I didn't have much time to play
The little games you asked me to,
I didn't have much time for you.

I'd wash your clothes.
I'd sew and cook,
But when you'd bring your picture book
And asked me please to share your fun,
I'd say, "A little later, son."

I'd tuck you in all safe at night
And hear your prayers, turn out the light,
Then tiptoe softly to the door . . .
I wish I'd stayed a minute more.

For life is short, the years rush past.
A little boy grows up so fast.
No longer is he at your side,
His precious secrets to confide.

The picture books are put away,
There are no longer games to play.
No good-night kisses, no prayers to hear;
That all belongs to yesteryear.

My hands, once busy, now are still
The days are long and hard to fill.
I wish I could go back and do
The little things you asked me to.[7]

*D*id Someone Say "Immovable"?

Earlier I mentioned that the beacon is an immovable landmark. However, in June 1999, North Carolina's most beloved landmark was moved. The Cape Hatteras Lighthouse was built in 1870 and had stood as sentry over what Alexander Hamilton dubbed "The Grave Yard of the Atlantic" because of the dangers to ships in that region. However, through the years, strong tides and shifting winds eroded the coastline, leaving the lighthouse only 120 feet away from the encroaching sea and in danger of toppling over into the surf.

The move came after twelve years of angry debate, several studies, and a lawsuit by those who wanted the lighthouse to remain where it was. In the end, state and federal officials concluded it must be moved. Twenty-three days after the tedious journey began, the Cape Hatteras Lighthouse reached the end of its 2,900-foot trek and now rests 1,600 feet from the water's edge. Safe for one hundred more years!

Why were the residents so passionate about the lighthouse's destiny? Why would Congress give $10 million to save it? Because some landmarks are worth fighting for. That's how I feel about motherhood and the family. They must be saved at all costs.

We live in a mobile society. We once sang, "Over the river and through the woods, to Grandmother's house we go." However, Grandmother's house is no longer "over the river and through the woods" but often across several state lines. We move. We relocate. We make new friends. We change schools. Corporate America thinks nothing of uprooting a family. How then can we give our children a sense of "coming home"?

One way is to establish family traditions. For example, each Valentine's Day I prepare the same menu: heart-shaped individual meat-loaf patties smothered in ketchup, mashed potatoes tinted pink, heart-shaped biscuits, and red velvet cupcakes. Every Christmas I prepare the same breakfast: egg and sausage casserole, cheese grits, and orange Danish rolls. Every year after final exams, we go out to lunch as a family to a favorite restaurant. Does my family tire of the sameness? No, they love it. It says "home."

Maybe your family will have to move one day. But as the beacon, where *you* are is home. That will never change. And when your children think of "home sweet home," they won't think about a street address. They'll think about you—the constant, guiding light, the landmark beacon that you are to them.

CHAPTER THREE

Glowing Features of a Beautiful Beacon

*W*hen I drive along the coast and come upon a lighthouse, I'm always caught a bit off guard with how monumentally gorgeous they are. Even though the map marks where the landmarks are stationed, I still feel a thrill when each one comes into view. I experience that same sensation when I see a mother nurturing her child. Mother love is nothing new, but each time I see it, my heart leaps. Lighthouses, like mothers, share certain common features; yet each one is beautiful and unique. A lighthouse's light—and a mother's—consistently burns bright, her stairs invite visitors to climb to greater heights, and her weathered exterior protects her inhabitants from the elements. But the most important feature is the oil in her lamp.

Keeping Oil in the Lamp

Recently, I stood looking at the Bodie Island Lighthouse, with her bold black-and-white horizontal stripes painted on her cement exterior. She is quite a flashy beacon, to say the least. Then I turned to look at the rough seas that were beating against the shore. I thought about the mariners who depended on the lighthouse's searching beam to lead them safely to land. What if she ran out of oil? What if she didn't shine? The ships were relying on her to be prepared and well supplied with oil.

Then I thought about my own life as a mother. Suppose I ran out of oil and my light grew dim—or worse, burned out altogether? What would happen to my little fleet?

The blessed mother in Proverbs 31:18 also had a lamp. Scripture says that "her lamp does not go out at night." I used to read that verse and think, *Doesn't this woman ever sleep!* But then I realized the description wasn't so much about her staying awake all night as it was about her lamp. She never let her oil supply run dry.

A lighthouse has one primary mission: to broadcast light so that a mariner can see the shore. Likewise, a mother is a beacon who displays light to guide her children through an ocean of choices. A mother's light is Jesus Christ, but she can't shine that light if her lamp runs dry.

Ephesians 5:18 says, "Be filled with the Spirit." That "be filled" is a present tense, continuous verb. It means to be filled daily and continually.[1] Interestingly, many times in Scripture the Holy Spirit is referred to as—you guessed it—oil!

How does a mother run out of oil? In Max Lucado's book *Just Like Jesus,* he tells a story that gives us a clue.

A lighthouse keeper who worked on a rocky stretch of coastline received oil once a month to keep his light burning bright. Not being far from the village, he had frequent guests. One night a woman needed oil to keep her family warm. Another night a father needed oil for his lamp. Then another needed oil to lubricate a wheel. All the requests seemed legitimate, so the lighthouse keeper tried to meet them all. Toward the end of the month, however, he ran out of oil and his lighthouse went dark, causing several ships to crash on the coastline. The man was reproved by his superiors. "You were given the oil for one reason," they said, "to keep the light burning."[2]

Mothers in the twenty-first century are tempted to meet every need that comes their way—and they are legion. But our primary job is to love the Lord, love our husbands, and nurture our children. All the other needs that scream for our attention, noble though they may be, must wait until we take care of our families.

Depleted Oil

What are some common oil depleters? Volunteering at school, helping in the community, counseling needy friends, taking care of other people's children, teaching Sunday school, singing in the choir for all three services, cooking meals for everyone who has a baby in your church, working on the missions committee, chairing the PTA, leading a neighborhood Bible study, being on the decorations committee for the school homecoming, making costumes for all the animals in the school play, being a Scout mother, den mother, and room mother (all at the same time), taking care of aging parents, hosting supper club once a month . . . Are you tired yet?

These activities are worthy, but we must realize that we can't do it all. Something—or someone—will suffer. Our oil will run out. When it does, we know who will suffer the most—first ourselves, then our families. We must learn how to say no without guilt.

In Mark 1:35, Jesus provides a good example of how to set priorities and get refueled. "Very early in the morning, while it was still dark, Jesus got up, left the house and went off to a solitary place, where he prayed." Jesus kept His oil refilled by meeting with God first thing in the morning and finding a quiet place to pray.

He also set His priorities for the day. Verses 36–38 go on to say, "Simon and his companions went to look for him, and when they found him, they exclaimed: 'Everyone is looking for you!' Jesus replied, 'Let us go somewhere else—to the nearby villages—so I can preach there also. That is why I have come.'"

Jesus had conducted a healing service the night before, and the people in Capernaum wanted more. Was continuing to minister to them a noble cause? Yes, but Jesus had set His priorities. He came to spread the Gospel, and that's what He continued to do. He wasn't distracted by the demands others placed on Him, but instead focused on God's will. And because He had spent time with God, He had new oil in His lamp and knew exactly where He was to shine.

Spending time with the Lord each day will help keep our priorities in order as well as provide fuel for us so that we can continue to be beacons burning brightly in our homes. We can ask Him to show us with fresh eyes what we should do. When we do, He guides our paths and instructs us in the way we should go (Psalm 32:8). He guides us in daily decisions. "Your ears will hear a voice behind you, saying, 'This is the way; walk in it'" (Isaiah 30:21).

What priority do your children have in your life? Most of us quickly would say they are right there at the top. But what do our calendars say? Where your treasure (your time) is, there will your heart be also. One of the dictionary's definitions of *priority* is "to prefer." Let's make sure we prefer our children.

When I was a teenager, I used to sing the little chorus, "Give me oil in my lamp, keep me burning, burning, burning. Give me oil in my lamp, I pray. Give me oil in my lamp, keep me burning, burning, burning. Keep me burning till the break of day." That song has taken on new meaning as I've become a beacon who desires never to let her lamp run dry.

Cleaning the Glass

I was sitting in a restaurant with several other mothers when the subject of movies came up. Two of the moms had seen a certain film, and the others were trying to decide if it was suitable for their teenage boys.

"Did it have any bad language?" Jean asked.

"I don't know," Candy replied. "I can't remember. Maybe a little."

"It had a lot!" Wendy said.

"What about sex scenes? Was there any of that in it?" Jean asked.

"No, I don't think so," Candy answered.

"You've got to be kidding," Wendy piped up. "Don't you remember . . ."

I thought, *Forget the boys! Why are you* women *watching that movie?*

The Bible says that the eye is the window to the soul, yet sometimes we allow the world's soot to build up in our souls until we can't see clearly.

The old-time lighthouse keeper had to refuel the light's flame with oil two to three times a night. But just as important as the oil supply was keeping soot from building up on the glass.

A mother whose children rise up and call her blessed must also keep the world's soot cleaned off by washing her soul's windows with the Word of God (Ephesians 5:26). Billy Graham once said that women should first "cultivate their souls that in turn they may cultivate the souls of their children."[3] Deuteronomy 6:6–7 says it this way, "And these words which I command you this day shall be upon your heart; and you shall teach them diligently to your children, and shall talk of them when you sit in your house, and when you walk by the way, and when you lie down, and when you rise" (RSV).

Did you catch that the commandments are to be upon "your heart"? We first have to know the Word before we can teach it to our children.

Elizabeth George, in her book *A Woman After God's Own Heart,* describes removing the soot as "the great exchange." She says:

> Away from the world and hidden from public view, I exchange my weariness for His strength, my weakness for His power, my darkness for His light, my problems for His solutions, my burdens for His freedom, my frustrations for His peace, my turmoil for His calm, my hopes for His promises, my afflictions for His balm of comfort, my questions for His answers, my confusion for His knowledge, my doubt for His assurance, my nothingness for His awesomeness, the temporal for the eternal, and the impossible for the possible.[4]

That's what I call a powerful window cleaner!

Climbing the Steps

As you climb the 268 steps of the Cape Hatteras Lighthouse, you'll see small portals, or windows, set in the cylindrical brick structure. At each level, the industrious climber can stop, catch her breath, and peer out toward the Atlantic Ocean. Each window offers a different view, and the closer the climber comes to the top, the more of the horizon's expanse she can see.

As mothers whose children rise up and call them blessed, we too are climbing a staircase, and at each stage of a child's life we experience a different view. Some days you might feel that you're going in circles and getting nowhere. On those days, exchange your vision of circles for the image of the spiraling, upward steps of the lighthouse.

So catch your breath, whisper a prayer, and keep climbing. Remember, the real view is at the top!

The following mock newspaper ads exemplify how our pace and perspective change as we climb ever higher.

Help Wanted—The Ideal Mother

For a Baby

Wanted: Easygoing, relaxed, loving type to care for infant. Should enjoy rocking, cuddling, be able to hold baby patiently for 20-minute feedings every three or four hours without fidgeting. Light sleeper, early riser. No degree necessary. Must take all shifts, seven-day week. No vacation unless can arrange to have own mother as temporary substitute. No opportunity to advance.

For 18-Month-Old
Wanted: Athlete in top condition to safeguard tireless toddler. Needs quick reflexes, boundless energy, infinite patience. ESP helpful. Knowledge of first aid essential. Must be able to drive, cook, phone, work despite constant distractions. Workday, 15 hours. No coffee or lunch breaks unless child naps. Would consider pediatric nurse with Olympic background.

For 3-Year-Old
Position Open: Expert in early childhood education to provide stimulating, loving, creative, individualized learning environment for preschooler. Should have experience in art, music, recreation, be able to speak one foreign language. Training in linguistics, psychology, and Montessori desirable. Two hours off five days a week when nursery school is in session and child is well.

For 6- to 12-Year-Old
Good Opportunity: For expert in recreation, camping, Indian arts, all sports. Should be able to referee. Must be willing to be den mother, room mother, block mother. Public relations skills essential. Should be able to deal effectively with teacher, PTA officers, other parents. Knowledge of sex education, new math required. Must have no objections to mud, insect collection, pets, neighbor's kids.

For 13- or 14-Year-Old
Job Available: For specialist in adolescent psychology, with experience in large-quantity cooking. Tolerance is chief requirement. Slight hearing loss helpful or must provide own ear plugs. Must be unflappable. Should be able to sense when presence is embarrassing to child and disappear.

After 18 Years As a Working Mother,
a Woman Is Qualified for Only One More Job:
Urgently Needed: Financier to provide money, clothes, music, wheels to collegian. No advice necessary. Position may last indefinitely. Ample time left to take income-producing work.

Like most want ads, some things were left out of these job descriptions:

1. A mother who has more than one child must usually hold down two or more of these posts simultaneously.
2. Those who handle the jobs best work themselves permanently out of a job.
3. There are greater rewards than anyone could ever imagine.[5]

Another way to view our progressive climb is to think about all the tasks a mother's hands undertake during the course of raising her children. On a shelf in my living room sits a black-and-white photograph of a young girl, taken in the early 1900s. Her hair is pulled back, with an oversized bow peeking from behind her head. Her dress is typical of the times. It has puffed sleeves and a brimming lace collar. She isn't smiling, and she appears to be somewhat awkward, timid, and, I daresay, even afraid. This is a picture of Grandmother Anderson on her wedding day. She was fourteen years old.

As I gaze at this amazing woman, who bore twelve children and miscarried eleven others, I'm always drawn to her hands. Hanging uncomfortably at her side, those hands seem much too large for her petite frame. "Anderson hands," my mother calls them. I surmise that God must have known this little lady would need a big heart and big hands to embrace all that life would send her way.

Like Grandmother Anderson, all of us mothers need big hearts and big hands. Our hands grip the bed rail in pain in the delivery room, then gently caress a newborn for the first time. Before long, those hands are changing diapers, washing bottoms and faces, cleaning spit-up, wiping tears, rocking sleepy heads, and placing babies in a crib. Then they are holding a toddler's chubby hand and grabbing him to keep him out of harm's way. Tossing a ball, preparing holiday dinners, setting a festive table, tying packages for birthday parties and Christmas presents keep those hands busy. Add to that coloring and cutting out shapes in workbooks, picking up leaves and bugs for collections, pushing a swing, and letting go of a bike as a child learns to pedal on his own. Then there's sewing party dresses and mending torn baseball jerseys, washing scraped knees, and spooning out medicine. Not to mention holding the sweaty palm of an awkward adolescent while dancing around the den, tying the knot of a necktie, and pinning on a boutonniere for a first party. The hands stay busy writing letters to children away at camp or folding in prayer asking for the Lord's protection while the children are away. Hands tightly grasp the steering wheel while chauffeuring children from one place to the next or grip the seat as a teen learns to drive. Hands wave good-bye as a son drives off to college, and hands adjust a cherished daughter's wedding veil. A mother's hands are loving hands, disciplining hands, grieving hands, protecting hands, and providing hands. They embrace the child and then, when a mother reaches the top of the lighthouse stairway, she lets him go.

Matt Osman's mother, Desiree, was on the top step of the stair when he wrote this tribute to his mother for his campus newspaper.

I Miss My Momma

Now settle down out there. I can already hear some of my friends starting the "your mom" jokes. Granted, I realize those never grow old, but I really do miss my mom. Besides, I'm secure enough to say it. Does my mom miss me? I can't imagine that she would. I'm sure she doesn't miss me beating on my sister or telling her that she is wrong. I remember when I first left for college. I wanted nothing more than to assert my own independence. "Oh, yeah, this is the life." Finally I was away from home, with no chores to do, the freedom to do what I wanted.

Call me a momma's boy, but the good old days when Mom used to fix me peanut butter and jelly sandwiches are starting to look better than ever. Granted, my memories are probably glorified accounts, but I love talking with my mom after dinner. I can never hear the same stories enough.

There was the time when as a 6-year-old I picked some chewed-up gum from a gravel ashtray at the mall. My mom, displaying an amazing quickness, threw me down and proceeded to dig it out of my mouth. Despite my kicking and screaming, this was only the beginning of a long line of battles I was destined to lose. Another time, my mother and I engaged in a battle of iron wills over the issue of potty training. Although I was only 2, I'm sure that my mother's love was severely tested that day. At the end of the day she literally threw me at my father when he walked in the door from work.

Like all familial relationships we had our fair share of ups and downs, the larger part of the downs coming because I had way too big a mouth for my own good. As convinced as my mom is that I have been scarred for life with some of our past warfare, I love her still. And the best part of it all is that I know she loves me. She gets worried when I am sick and prays for me when I am stressed out. She is deeply interested in my future and wants nothing but the best for her baby boy.

I hope to always hold that place in her heart. I remember watching the "Muppet Show" and "Monday Night Football" with her when I wouldn't sleep. My mom tells how she would hold me in her lap and with my little arms mimic the referee on television. One day I hope to hold my son and teach him how to signal a touchdown.

One of the best things about my mom is that she has never tried to hold me down so tight that I couldn't move. Never have I needed to cut the so-called apron strings to gain my freedom. In her infinite motherly wisdom, she gave me freedom rather than smothered me. When I left for college, my mom walked me to my car and said, "I don't want you to grow up, I just want you off the payroll." Gee, Mom, thanks for the sentiment. I don't enjoy being a sponge, but there's no sense in arguing the truth that I am. Sure, I worked my token summer job to pay for my "expenses," but it really boils down to the hard work and love of my parents who have blessed me with a college education.

I hope my mom realizes how much I love her. Even if all I ever bring home from school is dirty laundry and sleep deprivation. But even in this age of independence, I really do. I miss you, Momma.

See? The view from the top really is spectacular.

The Bricks and Mortar

County fairs are known for their various contests. At one particular fair, a pulling contest was used to determine who had the strongest horse. The first-place horse moved a sled weighing 4,500 pounds, and the second-place horse moved a sled that weighed 4,000. The owners were curious as to how much the two could pull if they worked together, so they hitched them up and added more weight to the sled. To everyone's surprise, the horses pulled 12,000 pounds.[6]

The word for combined strength, which was demonstrated in the two horses working together, is *synergism*. It means doing more together than one can do alone. What a beautiful picture of a marriage's power when the husband and wife work together. Even though this is a book for mothers,

I must point out that a strong marriage is the bricks and mortar of a sound structure, one that can withstand whatever the elements blow the beacon's way.

Harvard psychiatrist Armand M. Nicholi II noted:

> If any one factor influences the character development and emotional stability of an individual, it is the quality of the relationship he or she has with both parents. What has been shown to contribute most to the emotional development of the child is a close, warm, sustained, and continuous relationship with both parents.[7]

Children become very insecure when they see their parents fighting. Children can sense disunity. If we want to raise spiritually and emotionally healthy children, we must love their father second only to God.

But what if you are a single mother? Can you still have children who rise up and call you blessed? Absolutely. Is it difficult? Absolutely. But the Lord knows your every need. He knows that you have to do more in twenty-four hours than most. And He knows how to use the loneliness, pain, and sorrow of being single for the benefit of your family.

Your situation reminds me of a story. Years ago, shipbuilders used a specific process to make the main masts for merchant and military ships. The builders first climbed a hilltop and selected a sturdy tree that appeared to have a healthy root system. Then they cut down all the surrounding trees, exposing the chosen one to the forces of wind and rain. Over the years, the wind would blow against the lone tree. As it fought to stand its ground, it grew stronger and stronger until it was finally strong enough to be used as a ship's mast.[8]

Single mom, sink your roots deep into the soil. Be nourished by Jesus Christ. He will be a husband to you and a father to your children. And He will give you strength to stand firm in the storms of life and fashion you to become the mast for your family.

Recently, as I drove away from the Cape Hatteras Lighthouse, I thought about the seven stately beacons, standing tall, undaunted by decades of wind, rain, and crashing seas. I thought about my sisters in motherhood—the single moms and the mothers who have husbands by their sides—and I thought about myself. I left the coast with a new commitment to be a mother who is a shining beacon, whose lamp does not go out at night, and who keeps her glass clean from the world's soot. I'm nearing the top of the stairs in my journey. I'll admit, the view gets a little blurry from time to time, but it's not because of poor vision. It's because of tears as I wave Godspeed to my charge, who is pulling out to sea and on to new horizons. It has been quite a journey to the top, but, oh, what a view.

BRIGHT IDEAS

You can brighten the beacon for your children by:

- Evaluating the cost of having a job outside the home to see if it's cost effective (Be sure to include clothes, lunch, dry cleaning, child care, extra pediatrician visits, fast-food lunches and dinners, parking, gas, taxes, etc.)
- Considering working part-time, during the hours when children are at school
- Exploring the possibility of job sharing
- Working from home, such as data entry
- Attending your child's musical performances, sporting events, and special school assemblies
- Participating in field trips and school projects
- Taking pictures to remind you of the "steps" to the top of the lighthouse
- Chaperoning parties
- Making family dinners at home the norm, not the exception
- Having a snack with your children after school
- Meeting your child at the bus stop with a smile
- Waiting up for your teen when he or she is out at night, no matter how late it is
- Watching your child's favorite TV show with him or her
- Playing a board game together
- Establishing family traditions that say, "This is home"
- If your child is in a parade, standing on the street to watch him or her pass by
- Welcoming other children in your home to be a beacon to them
- Staying at home when your child is sick
- Volunteering to be a room mom at school

My mother was the making of me.

She understood me; she let me follow my bent.

—Thomas A. Edison

CHAPTER FOUR

Monica: A Beacon of a Mother

If ever a mother was a beacon, it was Monica, the mother of Augustine. From the time he was born, she prayed he would surrender his life to Christ and affect the world for God. However, Augustine's pagan father was just as zealous to lead young Augustine into sin as his mother was to introduce him to Christ.

Augustine himself said that, from the time he was born, he was "sealed with Christ's cross." However, he sidestepped God with the determination of a prizefighter.

In his early heathen years, Augustine attended the University of Carthage and received an excellent education in grammar, logic, literature, language, and oratory. During his years of higher education, he also experienced heavy doses of corruption, brothels, and friends in low places.

He graduated into a lifestyle of immorality, alcohol, and sexual promiscuity, living with one woman for fifteen years and fathering a child with her even though they never married. Eventually, he became a Manichean, which would compare to joining a modern-day cult.

Even though Augustine was living in apparent destitution of the soul, his mother continued to pray for him. Her light burned brightly with rays of hope, pointing him to Christ. Twice a day she added oil to her lamp as she went to church and cried out to the Lord on Augustine's behalf.

One day Monica approached a bishop who was bold in confronting others about their relationship to God and their need for salvation. She begged him to talk to Augustine, but he refused, saying that her son was unteachable. Still, as the bishop walked away, he replied, "It cannot be that the son of these tears should perish."

Shortly afterwards, Monica sensed that Augustine was planning to leave Carthage on a ship to Rome. When she confronted him at the dock, he denied it and said that he was only there to bid a friend farewell. However, the next morning, she discovered that her son had lied. He had indeed set sail for Rome and escaped her influence—or so it seemed. What she didn't realize was that, as her wayward son turned his eyes toward the shore of home, he pictured that faithful beacon, pointing him to the safety of Christ's harbor and the one true God.

Monica's prayers followed her son to Rome, and God continued to put people in his path to point him to the Savior. One day, while Augustine read one of Paul's letters in the Bible, the Holy Spirit touched his heart and opened his eyes. He knew God was speaking to him through those letters, and he committed his life to Jesus Christ.

Augustine went on to write more than one hundred books and one thousand sermons. The *Encyclopaedia Britannica* describes him as "the dominant personality of the Western Church of his time . . . generally recognized as having been the greatest thinker of Christian antiquity." His books *City of God* and *Confessions* are classics still read today. Sixteen hundred years later, the church continues to reap the benefits of this praying mother.

Shortly after Augustine became a Christian, Monica said that she felt her work on earth was accomplished. One week later, at the age of fifty-six, she died.

In one of his prayers Augustine wrote the following about his mother, "She poured out her tears and her prayers all the more fervently, begging you [God] to speed your help and give me light in my darkness."[1] Another entry reads:

My mother, your faithful servant, wept to you for me, shedding more tears for my spiritual death than other mothers shed for the bodily death of a son. For in her faith and in the spirit which she had from you she looked down on me as dead. You heard her and did not despise the tears which streamed down and watered the earth in every place where she bowed her head in prayer.[2]

Monica remained a beacon of light, a visible sentinel, pointing her son to the safe harbor of Christ's arms. And Augustine, indebted to his mother for her unceasing intercession, rose and called her blessed.

Her love is like an island
In life's ocean, vast and wide.
A peaceful quiet shelter
From the wind and rain, and tide.
'Tis bound on the north by Hope,
By Patience on the west.
By tender Counsel on the south,
And on the east by Rest.
Above is like a beacon light,
Shining Faith, and Truth, and Prayer;
And through the changing scenes of life,
I find a haven there.

—Author Unknown[3]

My mother made a brilliant impression upon my childhood life.
She shone for me like the evening star—I loved her dearly.

—Winston Churchill

For me, a line from mother is more efficacious than all the homilies preached in Lent.

—Henry Wadsworth Longfellow

SECTION TWO

Be a
Listener

$\mathcal{L}$isten with Your Whole Being

Each letter in the word "blessed" builds on the one before, not only to spell the word but also to be a mother whose children rise and call her blessed. Imagine, if you will, wooden alphabet blocks being stacked one on top of another. The first block is B—the blessed mother is a Beacon. She's a guiding light and a landmark in her children's lives. Next, she's a Listener, attentive to the changing needs, hopes, and desires of her family. She "listens" with her whole being.

Unfortunately, research shows that stay-at-home moms spend about 30 minutes a day conversing with their kids, and mothers who work outside the home spend fewer than 11 minutes. Now, if we assume that half of that time the parent is doing the talking, listening time drops to 15 minutes for the stay-at-home mom and 5.5 minutes for the working mom.[1] I've always been taught that as long as I'm talking, I'm not learning. If I want to be a good student of my child, I need to listen to what he is saying.

In the 1960s, Art Linkletter captured Americans' hearts in a television segment called "Kids Say the Darnedest Things." Each week he asked four children perched on stools in the studio a simple question. Then he handed them the microphone while millions of adults sat back and listened. The kids' answers were entertaining, informative, and more imaginative than any scriptwriter could create. Mr. Linkletter noted, "There's a vast gulf between the world of children and our own. Every time we bridge that gulf—even if it's only for a moment—we recapture some of the freshness and spontaneity that makes life worth living."[2]

Let's explore different ways that the blessed mom can bridge that gulf and strengthen her children's hearts—and add some spontaneity and laughter to her own.

How do you tune in to your child's needs? It takes more than using your ears. You must listen with your whole being: eyes, ears, face, lips, mind, and heart. This is no easy task, but who said being a blessed mom is?

Listen with Your Eyes

Ross Campbell in his book *How to Really Love Your Child* states that most parents love their children but don't know how to show it. Consequently, many children don't feel genuinely and unconditionally loved.[3]

How does a mother show love? By focusing attention on her child. That means putting down that dustcloth, turning to face the child, and bending down, if necessary, to make eye contact.

How do you feel when you're trying to have a conversation with someone but that person won't look at you? You probably feel uncomfortable, as if she isn't really listening or she can't be trusted. How do I feel when I'm talking to my darling husband during a televised football game? Even if he pushes the mute button, that's not enough. I want him to look at me. After all, who's more important, the Steelers or *moi?*

Imagine how our children feel when we keep working while they're trying to tell us something important to them. We tend to make direct eye contact only when a child performs especially well (to express our approval) or especially poorly (to make our point, to reprimand, or to criticize). But a blessed mom is one who listens on a regular basis with her eyes. And remember this, if we don't listen to our young children, they won't talk to us when they're teens.

Exactly when does the need to listen with our eyes begin? The obvious answer is at the time the child starts to talk, but actually we should start months before that.

An infant focuses his eyes around two to four months of age. One of the first images that holds his attention is the human face, in particular, the eyes. We've all seen an infant panning the room for his mother. What is the child asking when he searches for his mom?

"Do you love me, Mommy?"

When, with listening eyes, she locks onto her child's eyes, she is answering, "Yes." Nothing is more beautiful than a mother holding her infant, their eyes locked on each other in a compassionate gaze. This is the first form of communication.

Now, suppose the mother just speaks to the infant from across the room and doesn't look into the baby's eyes. The infant's need to be assured of Mom's love is just as unsatisfied as a wife's need is unmet when she finds herself competing for her husband's attention with the Atlanta Braves in the World Series.

Listen with Your Ears

Telling someone to listen with her ears seems redundant. But the blessed mom must not let her children's words go in one ear and slip out the other. She must tune in with her radar and all the other homing devices God has provided.

I was struck by an article in the *Charlotte Observer* about a friend for hire. Joanne Ivancich was described as a friend for hire, earning as much as $500 a month to sit and listen to whatever a person wanted to talk about. She is called a "personal development coach," who helps people focus and make decisions. Basically, she receives payment for two things: asking good questions and telling the truth. The *Observer* noted that *Newsweek* referred to this type of coaching as "part consultant, part motivational speaker, part therapist and part rent-a-friend."[4]

An ad in a Kansas newspaper read, "I will listen to you, without comment for thirty minutes for $5." The person who placed the ad received ten to twenty calls per day.[5] No doubt most of the calls were from adults, but the need to have a listening ear begins much earlier. And the value of listening to our children is immeasurable, worth much more than $5 for thirty minutes.

God is aware of our propensity to hear but not to really listen. In Matthew 13:14 Jesus says, "You will keep on hearing, but will not understand; and you will keep on seeing, but will not perceive" (NASB). He also stated what happens when we do listen well. "Blessed are your eyes, because they see; and your ears, because they hear" (verse 16 NASB). There's that word "blessed" again!

We never outgrow the need to have a listening ear. Our children may not be able to hire a friend, but they will find someone. If we're smart, we'll make sure that someone is their mom.

Listen with Your Facial Expressions

Charles Swindoll tells a story about how our facial expressions encourage or discourage conversation. During his days as president, Thomas Jefferson and his companions were traveling across the country on horseback. They came to a river that had risen past its banks because of a recent downpour. The swollen stream had also washed away the bridge, which meant each man had to ford the river on horseback, fighting for his life against the rapid current. The possibility of death threatened each rider, causing a traveler who was not part of their group to step aside to watch.

After several had plunged in and made it to the other side, the stranger asked President Jefferson if he might ride with him across the river. The president agreed without hesitation. The man climbed on, and shortly thereafter the two of them made it safely to the other side. As the stranger slid off the horse's back onto dry ground, one in the group asked him, "Tell me, why did you select the president?" The man was shocked, admitting he had no idea it was the president who had helped him. "All I know," he said, "is that on some of your faces was written the answer 'No,' and on some of them was the answer 'Yes.' His was a 'yes' face."[6]

I understand just what the fellow meant. Although much less was at stake, when I ventured off to a local fabric store to purchase material for drapes, the idea of having a yes face was vividly illustrated to me. I approached a salesclerk and asked for a sample swatch. She didn't make eye contact, and her face said, "You're bothering me with your silly request. Can't you see I'm busy!" I left, feeling frustrated.

Three days later, I returned to the same store and was greeted by a different salesperson, Mildred. She helped me pick out my fabric, listened to me think aloud, nodded her head at the appropriate times, and gave me so much attention I felt as if I were the only person she had to wait on that day. The next day, I returned to the store, asked for Mildred, and purchased thirty-five yards of fabric. Mildred had a yes face and a commission to prove it.

What kind of face do you have? Is it a face that makes your children feel it's OK to say whatever they think? Is it the kind of face that communicates no request is too silly and no question too insignificant? If we have a no face, chances are our children will stop coming to talk to us and look for others who care enough to listen.

Listen with Your Lips

How does a person listen with her lips? After all, isn't it by keeping our lips zipped that we truly listen? Well, not necessarily. One key way to show you're listening is to *complete the loop* in the conversation with comments that show you're engaged. For example, if a child says, "I didn't like math class today," then the mother would complete the loop by responding,

"Really? What didn't you like about it?" Now the child knows Mom is paying attention and wants to know more.

Here's another example:

Child: "Sally is such a jerk. She really makes me mad."

Mother: "Really? What did she do to make you so angry?"

Child: "She told everybody on the playground that I was a baby because I couldn't go to any movie except ones rated G."

If either of the child's opening sentences was followed by silence from the parent, it would be translated, "She's not even listening to me," or, "She doesn't care what I'm saying. I'm going to call Sara when I get home. She'll talk to me."

In the second illustration, another way to close the lines of communication would be for the parent to say, "You're being ugly by calling Sally a jerk. You shouldn't feel that way about her." Judging a child's comments right off the bat is a sure conversation stopper, but following her remark with a question invites her to say more.

Still another sure way to stop the flow of sharing is to betray a confidence. What may seem like a harmless piece of information to us might be a "big deal" to our children. If Sally lets her mom in on the secret that she thinks Bob in her math class is really handsome, and then that mom tells her friends because she thinks the comment is cute, Sally could be devastated. That careless mom will not be privy to many secrets in the future.

Listen with Your Mind

Listening is no easy task. You have to tune in with your ears, direct your eyes, and respond with your facial expression and lips. But perhaps the most important ingredient to listening to your child is that he has to talk! And one of the best ways to cultivate conversation is to ask good questions. Notice I said *good* questions. This is an art form, a discipline, and an exercise of the mind.

Jesus was a master at asking pertinent questions. He is referred to as a healer and teacher, but He was also an active listener. He asked questions of lawyers, invalids, mothers, politicians, fishermen, rabbis, demons, a blind man, Roman officers, a leper, and the disciples. In the Sermon on the Mount alone, He asked fourteen questions.

He asked the woman caught in adultery, "Where are your accusers?" (John 8:10 TLB). He asked the scribes, "Which is easier: to say to the paralytic, 'Your sins are forgiven,' or to say, 'Get up, take your mat and walk'?" (Mark 2:9).

Obviously, since Jesus is omniscient, He knows everything. He didn't ask questions to gather information. Instead, He used questions to get people to think and many times to help them come to conclusions. We can use questions in the same way with our children.

Robert C. Crosby in his book *Now We're Talking! Questions That Bring You Closer to Your Kids* notes that "questions are one of the most effective yet perhaps most underused tools in a parent's toolbox today. Just five minutes of expressing interest in your child will do more to build your relationship with him or her than five months of trying to get him or her interested in you."7 This echoes the old adage "To be interesting, you must be interested."

Mrs. McVey was a grandmother who complained to my husband that her two grandchildren showed little interest in her. They never came by to visit or called to see how she was doing. Curious, Steve took Mrs. McVey by to visit the twosome. Sure enough, when they answered the door, the grandkids weren't very excited to see her but dutifully gave her a hug and invited her in. They all quietly sat in the room, the grandmother waiting for the ungrateful kids to show a little love and respect, and the kids waiting for the visit to be over.

That's when Steve decided to try a little experiment by asking the younger boy some questions. "Peter, how's baseball going this year?"

"Fine."

"Who's your best hitter?"

"Joe. He's really good," Peter answered with a tiny ray of enthusiasm.

"I heard you had a double play the other day. What happened?"

With that, Peter began to warm up. His countenance changed from boredom to enthusiasm. He became so chatty that Steve could hardly slip a word in edgewise. Peter was talking about his two favorite subjects: baseball and himself.

The conversation coasted smoothly on, with Steve asking questions and the kids telling him everything he wanted to know about their lives. They didn't want him to leave. Steve was "cool" because he was interested in them, and they knew it.

Their grandmother could have been dubbed "the coolest grandma around" had she shown interest in her grandchildren instead of expecting them to be interested in her. Kids don't work that way.

All mothers of adolescents have had this conversation with their children:

"How was your day at school?"

"Fine."

"What did you do?"

"Nothin'."

"Do you have much homework?"

"No."

If you've ever grown frustrated with this monosyllabic lingo, maybe it's not the answers that are the problems but the questions that need some improvement.

We have two types of questions to choose from: closed and open. A closed question is one that can be answered with one word: "Good," "Bad," "OK," "Yes," "No." For example, "Did you have a good day?" "Did you like your dinner?" "Was the math test hard?" These conversation stoppers reinforce the idea that it's hard to listen if no one is talking.

An open question is one that draws out the person and requires a more thoughtful answer. "What was the best thing that happened at school today?" "Who did you sit with at lunch?" "If you could do anything for God, and money were no object, what would that be?" As your child begins to talk in response to your open question, you need to complete the loop with follow-up questions, showing that you're tuned in and want to know more. Since you're a blessed mother who attends activities such as plays and sporting events, you have a rich storehouse of question material to draw from. As Robert Crosby said,

> Ambassadors use questions to build bridges between countries that are oceans apart. Teachers use questions to build bridges to their students. Spouses use questions to build intimacy with one another. Managers use questions to cultivate teamwork and productivity among employees. Wise parents use questions to bridge the generation divide with their children, whether en route to nursery school or on the way home from a high school soccer game.[8]

After one of Steven's basketball games, we went over the game, play-by-play, on the ride home.

"Did you see Anthony's three-point shot? That was awesome!" I commented.

"Can you believe that guy elbowed me, and the ref didn't call a foul? That made me hot!"

"Yeah, I saw that. It was a cheap shot, but I'm proud of you for not losing your temper. That would have been hard for me. You did a great job blocking number 23 in the third quarter. Which one of the guys was the hardest to cover?"

Can you feel the excitement? Can you see the opportunity that awaits you as you discuss the events you attended with your child?

Notice that I didn't use this time to coach him on what he could have done better. That's probably one of the biggest mistakes parents make as they talk to their kids. Would you want someone to always tell you how to do something better and to point out all your weaknesses? I wouldn't. If that's what happens on your car ride home, expect some quiet passengers. As a matter of fact, don't be surprised if your little Johnny wants to ride home with his friend Charley and his cool mom who asks great questions and points out each player's awesome moves.

Questions draw in people. They are an invitation to relationship.

One day a friend of mine went on a trip with her son. At first the radio was on, but then her son reached over and turned it off. "Mom, let's just talk awhile."

If this happened to you (talk about being blessed!), what would you say? Here are a few questions to get you started.

1. What do you think heaven looks like?
2. What does Dad do at work?
3. Who do you see as the most Christlike among everyone you know?
4. What do you think your wife (husband) will be like?
5. If you were going to spend one year on a desert island and could only take three things, what would they be?
6. Who is your favorite aunt or uncle, and why do you like him or her so much?
7. What sounds and smells do you think Joseph and Mary experienced in the stable on Christmas night?
8. What is the nicest thing I ever did for you?
9. When was a time I hurt your feelings?
10. When was a time you were really mad at me?
11. If people followed the Golden Rule, think of all the things we wouldn't need. Can you make a list?
12. If you could be in a movie, which character would it be? Would you be a character who's already in the movie, or would you be someone else?
13. How is love different for a Christian couple than it is in the movies?
14. What's the difference between being smart and being wise?
15. What's your favorite outfit?
16. What's the hardest part about being _____ (fill in your child's age)?
17. What's your favorite childhood memory?
18. When you pray, how do you picture God?
19. What's your favorite Bible verse? Why do you like it?
20. If you could be an animal for a day, which one would you be?
21. If you could travel in a time machine, what time period would you visit?
22. What person in history would you like to visit?
23. What's the most important decision you'll ever make?

Of course the list is endless—but that's the best part. Strengthen your arsenal of questions by coming up with your own list. Remember, there's a difference between inquiring to get to know your child and interrogating to solve a crime. Check your attitude and your motives. It will make the difference between meaningful conversation and defensive reactions.

Listen with Your Heart

Many times in our children's lives we'll need to listen with our hearts. God has given women a special gift called intuition. We just "know" things. Come on, you know what I mean.

When it comes to child rearing, we have to do more than listen with our ears, eyes, lips, faces, and minds. We must engage our hearts. We must listen to the feelings first and later focus on the information.

Just a few miles from my home in Charlotte, farmers grow wonderfully sweet South Carolina peaches. When the young peach tree begins to bear fruit, many times the immature branches are too fragile to bear all the weight. To keep the fruit-laden branches from snapping, the farmer props them up with stakes.

The same is true for our children. When their load becomes too heavy and we sense they are about to break, we need to prop up their branches so that the fruit will ripen to maturity. But to do that, we have to be aware of what's going on in their lives by listening with our hearts. They may not come right out and tell us when life gets too complicated or their spirits are sagging. That's when we need to read between the lines.

Is your child acting up in a way that's out of character? Maybe she is crying out for more attention from Mom. Is your teen sullen and spending too much time alone in his room? Maybe he is crying out because he is feeling rejected at school. Is the baby especially fussy even though the doctor says, "Sorry, Mrs. Jones, nothing is wrong, and there's no ear infection." Maybe your baby is saying, "I sense you're uptight, Mom. Hey, what's wrong with *you?*"

When my son was in the seventh grade, he was taking advanced math, advanced English, advanced science, and Latin. He was playing on a school sports team for the first time, and he didn't arrive at home until six at night. Nothing was going well. He struggled to finish his schoolwork because he was exhausted each evening. A few times he had worked hard on an assignment only to find he had done the wrong page. Latin was Greek to him, and I saw no sign that he was going to catch on anytime soon.

One day after practice, I heard him in the shower crying out to God, "Lord, I'm not good at anything. Just help me be good at something. Just one thing."

It broke my heart. Actually, he was great at many things, but his emotions were on overload. His branches were about to break. I met with the principal, and we dropped one of the advanced courses (Latin). Also, Steven was encouraged when one of his teachers, who knew that he was having a hard time, sent us this note:

Dear Mr. and Mrs. Jaynes,

Steven has been doing excellent work in science. His name has been at the top of the list on recent tests and quizzes. No doubt he told you about his perfect score on our last test. He is a fine young man. I would love a room full of Stevens!

Best regards,

Mrs. Connie Roads

That teacher listened with her heart. She knew that Steven was discouraged. She knew that, when we received her note, we would share it with him. It proved to be a turning point in his year. Yes, I took him out of Latin and tried to lighten the load where I could, but the teacher's encouraging words turned his year around. And for that, I rise up and call her blessed.

Adolescence is a time to cut those apron strings and to encourage more independence. But the job's not over yet! This, more than any other time, is when we have to be on guard. As the fruit of adulthood begins to sprout on the immature branches and weighs them down, we must be aware of when our children need our support. Galatians 6:2 says, "Bear one another's burdens" (NASB). The word *burdens* might more aptly be translated "overburdens."[9] These are not everyday burdens such as forgetting homework or leaving the lunch box on the kitchen table . . . again. Letting children suffer the consequences for such behavior is merely teaching responsibility. An overburden is when the pressures of growing up and life in general are more than our children are ready to bear. That's when we listen with our hearts and share the load.

Listen

When I ask you to listen to me
And you start giving advice,
You have not done what I asked.

When I ask you to listen to me
And you begin to tell me why I shouldn't feel that way,
You are trampling on my feelings.

When I ask you to listen to me
And you feel you have to do something
To solve my problem,
You have failed me,
Strange as that may seem.

So please listen and just hear me.
And if you want to talk,
Wait a minute for your turn;
And I'll listen to you.

—Author Unknown

CHAPTER SIX

*T*ime
to Listen

*Y*ou know how hard it is to listen to your children when the washing machine is spinning, the vacuum cleaner is roaring, the baby is crying, the phone is ringing, the dog is barking, and the TV is blaring—all at the same time. We live in a noisy world, and opportunities to find quiet so that you can listen are rare. However, listening moments do occur throughout the day, if we have ears to hear.

*C*ar Time

I love the bumper sticker that reads, "If a mother's place is in the home, then why am I always in the car?" In this new millennium, the car has become our home away from home. We eat in the car, put our makeup on in the car, and talk on the phone in the car. Since this is the place we're going to spend so much of our time, let's practice being a blessed mother in our home on wheels.

All through Steven's years in school, I never participated in a car pool. I know my neighbors thought I was silly, and it did seem a little strange to pull out of the driveway at the same time as another mother, to head for the same drop-off point. However, I was unwilling to give up that precious time in the car before and after school when I could talk alone with my son.

Those were some of the best conversations we ever had, and the time I spent in traffic taking Steven to and from school provided treasures in my storehouse of memories. When I picked him up from school in the afternoon, I wanted him to know this was the best part of my day, and I heard about his day while it was fresh on his mind. If his mood was sullen, I listened first with my eyes, then with my ears as I coaxed him to talk, and then with my heart as we sat in silence. Traffic time can be a blessing.

I remember one particular ride home when Steven was fifteen. He was telling me about some of the boyfriend-girlfriend relationships at school. I asked open-ended questions, and he elaborated on his answers. At one point he stopped midsentence and said, "I can't believe I'm telling you this!" That's when I knew I was experiencing the rewards of good listening—and not just because I was listening that day but because I'd been listening to Steven for fifteen years and had established a relationship of trust and caring. It didn't happen overnight. But it did happen. I'm still listening today.

Do you have to run errands? Take a child along. Pick one child and use the time to listen to him or her. You'll be amazed how your children open up when they are with Mom alone.

Do you have to take a road trip? Pick a child to take along. Turn off the radio. Put away the CDs. Outlaw headphones in the car.

As you drive your child from place to place, utilize the time to steer him or her in the right direction down the road of life.

Bedtime

"Tell me, what was the worst part of this day? Now, what was the best part?" I used to ask those two questions on a regular basis at bedtime. What a wonderful time to listen to your children, after you've kissed their heads and tucked them into bed. Kids will do just about anything to postpone going to sleep. So take a moment, sit on the edge of the bed, and listen to what they have to say. Tune in to what they are thinking, catch up on their day, detect concerns, and answer questions. Let them tell you a bedtime story about what's going on in their hearts and minds.

Voltaire said, "The road to the heart is the ear," and bedtime is the perfect time to travel down that road.

Playtime

Studies have shown that boys in particular tend to talk more when they are engaged in a physical activity. I must say that I became very proficient at army men, Lego building blocks, and Playmobil. Days of pushing around toy cars and trucks, making tents under the Ping-Pong table, eating lunch in the tree fort, creating puppet shows, and playing general store were times when I listened while I played. These were deposits in my son's love account that continued to draw compound interest into the teenage years. Again, building the relationship is key when it comes to being a blessed mother who is a listener.

Mealtime

A study was conducted with several families who had raised "successful" children. The researchers analyzed what the families did and found that a common thread ran through each family: They ate at least one meal together daily.

Some of the best conversations occur around the dinner table. Throughout Scripture, we see meaningful table talk: Jesus went home with Zacchaeus for dinner, He taught the disciples while fish roasted over an open fire, and He allowed questions and answers during the Last Supper. In the Old Testament, we see Queen Esther inviting the king to dinner before she made her request to save the Jews. The remembrance of Passover focused on a meal, and kings often invited their advisers to join them at the dinner table each evening.

For generations, dinner was a time when families came together after a day of scattered activities and demands. However, today, soccer, ballet, gymnastics, Tae Kwon Do, PTA, and so on are competing against the priceless treasure of family time.

Part of the way we can fight against the encroachment of all these activities on mealtime is to make sure dinner is something our children look forward to. I'm not talking about the feast on the table but about the feast of our hearts, as we enjoy time together. This is not the moment to settle family disputes and administer discipline. Instead it's a time to relax and recount what's going on in each other's life.

Notice when the resurrected Christ chose to discipline Peter, who had denied Him three times before the Crucifixion. It wasn't during the meal Jesus was sharing with the disciples but after the group had enjoyed eating together (John 21). We need to fill the dinner hour not with gripes and complaints but with pleasant conversation, focusing on each other and what we're eating—not on what's eating us.

To be a blessed mother, listen at mealtime rather than watch TV. At my home, the TV isn't allowed near our dining table. But in many homes, Peter Jennings, Tom Brokaw, and Dan Rather join the family for dinner each night. I'd much rather listen to news about why Mrs. Moore's math test was too hard, who Mike is taking to the senior prom, or how far Casey got on the monkey bars at recess.

A Tale of Two Moms and a Kid

Just in case you ever doubted the importance of lending a listening ear to your child, here's a cautionary tale about a couple of moms and their kids.

Karen:

I remember a time when I came home from cheerleading tryouts my junior year in high school. I hadn't made the squad. I was number seven, and they picked six girls. One of my long-time rivals made it instead of me. I was crushed. I walked into the kitchen where my mom was preparing dinner. I was crying—bawling, actually. My mother's response was something like, "You need to stop crying about it. You can try out again next year." No hug, no comforting words. Instead, she continued with what she was doing as I ran to my room and cried. I was so hurt.

Later in life I had the benefit of going to a counselor with my mom a few times. During one session, I brought up the cheerleading scenario. My mother didn't even remember it. We did a role-play in our session, and I pretended I was she, and she was I. I was able to show her what I needed at that time. She ended up crying when she realized how her lack of listening to my needs had scarred me even into adulthood.

Jessi:

I had a wonderful mother growing up. Unfortunately, I never fully realized it at the time. God blessed me so much with her that I can never repay Him. Almost every night she would sit with me before I went to bed and listen to my sorrows. You see, I wasn't a popular child, and I certainly wasn't outgoing or social. So I was teased mercilessly every day by the other kids, and I had nobody to vent my frustrations on. Nobody, that is, but my mom.

She would tuck me in each night, and never once do I remember her wincing when I said, "Mommy, can we talk?" I would keep her up well past ten with my ongoing woes, dreams, and worries, which I felt I couldn't trust anyone but her to hear. I vented my frustration about the kids at school, worried about my grades—which were never very good until high school, spoke to her about how badly I wanted to be a famous author someday, asked question after question after question. . . . She would sit there beside me on my bed, smiling and nodding and letting me cry on her shoulder or offering advice. She was my security blanket, my sounding board, my shoulder to cry on, and my counselor. She was everything I needed to make it through each day. All I had to do was think of her waiting for me at home, and I knew I could face anything, just like she always told me I could.

A Kid:

Dear Folks,

Thank you for everything, but I'm going to Chicago and try to start some kind of new life for myself. You ask me why I did those things that got me in trouble, why I gave you so much static while I was at home. The answer is easy for me to give you. But I don't know if you'll understand. Remember when I was about 6 or 7 years old and I used to want you just to listen to me? I remember all the nice things you gave me for Christmas and my birthday, and I was really happy with those things for about a week, but the rest of the time during the year all I wanted was you. I just wanted you to listen to me like I was somebody who felt things. Because I remember when I was young, I felt things. But you always were busy. You never seemed to have time. Mom, you're a wonderful cook and you always have everything so clean, and you were tired from doing all those things that made you busy. But you know something, Mom? I would have liked crackers and peanut butter just as well if you'd only sat down with me a while during the day and said to me, "Tell me all about it. Maybe I can help you understand." I think that all the kids who are doing so many things that grownups are tearing out their hair worrying about are really looking for is somebody that will have time to listen a few minutes, and who will really treat them as they would a grownup who might be useful to them, you know. Well, if anybody asks you where I am, just tell them I've gone looking for somebody with time 'cause I've got a lot of things I want to talk about.

Love to you all,
Your son[1]

TWENTY-TWO WAYS TO
REALLY LISTEN TO YOUR CHILDREN

1. Be patient.
2. Don't complete their sentences.
3. Let them finish, even if it seems they are rambling.
4. Don't interrupt.
5. Face your child and make eye contact.
6. Lean forward, if you're seated, to show you're interested.
7. Take advantage of passive moments such as watching a video, listening to music, or sitting on the edge of their bed when tucking them in at night.
8. Take your children along on errands.
9. Ask good questions but avoid the word "why."
10. Ask their opinion about something that happened to you.
11. Don't jump to conclusions.
12. Don't change the subject. Make verbal responses such as "I see," "Really," "Uh-huh," to show that you're paying attention.
13. Avoid telling them not to feel a certain way. ("Don't worry about it." "Don't cry.")
14. Turn off the TV.
15. Put down the mop, newspaper, or dishtowel.
16. Encourage them to tell you more. "What else did he say?" "What did he do next?"
17. When they are telling of a struggle, rephrase and repeat what you heard. "What I hear you saying is that you feel I'm being unfair by not letting you go to the concert on a school night."
18. Don't always point out grammar mistakes but listen for the point of the story.
19. Let the phone ring if your child is in the middle of telling you about an event in his life.
20. Anytime your child starts to talk or ask a question, consider it an invitation to which you should RSVP.
21. Don't glance at your watch while they are talking.
22. God gave you two ears and one mouth for a good reason. Listen twice as much as you talk!

How are you doing in listening to your child? See if you can answer the following questions.

Who's your child's favorite teacher?

What's the most hurtful thing anyone has ever said to him or her?

What does he or she fear most about going to high school? College?

What are his or her friends like?

Who's his or her best friend?

Who does he or she admire most?

What's his or her favorite music group?

If you struggled to answer those questions, it's never too late to start learning. Become a student of your child. A mother whose children one day rise up and call her blessed is a Listener.

CHAPTER SEVEN

Susanna Wesley:
A Listening Mother

Susanna Wesley was born in 1669 in London, the twenty-fifth and last child of the Reverend Samuel Annesley and his wife. At nineteen years of age, Susanna married Samuel Wesley and, over the next nineteen years, averaged one child per year. For her ten surviving children, she was a diligent, disciplined, and faithful mother who instilled godly values and a hunger to know Christ.

We could talk about Susanna Wesley in any section of this book. She was a beacon, a listener, an encourager, a self-esteem builder, a seed sower, an example setter, and a diligent mother. But one of the most amazing characteristics of this blessed mother was that she found time to listen amid the hustle and bustle of a household teeming with children.

She devoted her life to the spiritual and academic training of her children and set aside a room in her home as the schoolroom. There she held "class" each day from nine to twelve, then again from two until five. The children learned to read by age five, using the Bible as their primary text. They began each day with psalms and prayers and ended it with psalms and singing. Each child read a book in the Old and New Testament every day. She also taught them Latin, writing, poetry, and music. But most important, she taught discipline, respect, and a reverence for God.

Before you close this book and say, "Forget it! I have only two children and can barely keep up," bear in mind that she did have a servant or two. But her disciplined lifestyle aided her to accomplish her primary goal: to raise godly children.

Susanna knew the value of focused attention and spent quality time alone with each of her youngest eight children still living at home. On Mondays, she spent time with Millie, Tuesdays with Henry, Wednesdays with Nancy, Thursdays with Jacky, Fridays with Parry, Saturdays with Charles, and Sundays with Emelia and Sukey. She wanted to do more than be her children's teacher. She wanted to know them intimately. She wanted to listen to them with her ears, eyes, heart, face, lips, and mind.

What were the dividends of her invested time? Perhaps her best-known children are John, a renowned evangelist and theologian who preached more than 42,000 sermons and wrote 233 books, and Charles, who wrote more than 8,000 hymns. Together, they founded Methodism and led a revival in the Church of England by teaching that salvation is through grace alone, through Christ alone. The two brothers traveled more than a quarter of a million miles to spread the Gospel of Jesus Christ.

John rose up and called his mother blessed when he said, "I learned more about Christianity from my mother than from all the theologians of England. My mother was the source from which I derived the guiding principles of my life."[1]

MOTHER'S DAY PROCLAMATION

Whereas the service rendered the United States by the American mother is the greatest source of the country's strength and admiration; and whereas we honor ourselves and the mothers of America when we do anything to give emphasis to the home; and whereas the American mother is doing so much for good government and humanity, we declare that the second Sunday of May will henceforth be celebrated as Mother's Day.

—Presidential Proclamation 1914

A MOTHER'S DAY CONFESSION

Mother's Day—
A day spent praising me.
If only I could measure up
To the "Super Mom" I'm supposed to be!

I long to be that myth
Of every young one's dreams,
But I'm just ME with all my flaws,
Struggling with self-esteem.

I worry about the mistakes I've made.
I wonder how they'll survive.
"In spite of me," I'm told they'll flourish,
Perhaps they'll even thrive.

Throughout their days I've been there,
Bandaging all the vital parts.
Dear Lord, for the times I've failed them,
Please heal their fractured hearts.

And though I am not worthy
Of these praises I confess,
Because You've blessed me richly,
In Your strength, I'll do my best.

—Nancee Skipper[2]

My mother was the most beautiful woman I ever saw. . . . All I am I owe to my mother. . . . I attribute all my success in life to the moral, intellectual, and physical education I received from her.

—George Washington

It was a memory that met us everywhere, for every person in town, from the highest to the lowest, seemed to have been so impressed by my mother's character and life that they constantly reflected some portion of it back on us.

—Harriet Beecher Stowe

SECTION THREE

Be an Encourager

CHAPTER EIGHT

*B*ecoming Your Child's Chief Cheerleader

*M*y nephew Stu began running on his school cross-country team when he was in the eighth grade. Since we lived two hundred miles from his home, I couldn't watch him run at his meets, but I heard the main attraction at Stu's races was not the runners but his enthusiastic mother.

When Stu was a high school senior, his team came to my hometown for a state competition. If you've ever attended a cross-country race, you know it's not exactly a spectator sport. Runners line up on the starting mark. A man fires a gun for the race to begin. Then the participants disappear down a trail in the woods, only to reappear some sixteen minutes later.

Before the race, our family stood on the sidelines, watching legs stretch, backs bend, and arms swing as the runners worked to warm up. Seventy anxious young men clustered around the starting line in ready position. The shot was fired into the air, and the herd of boys began their 3.1-mile jaunt through the woods.

As soon as Stu's foot left the starting position, his mother, Pat, picked up her thirty-six-inch megaphone and yelled louder than any woman I've ever heard. "GO, STU!" She cheered not once but at ten-second intervals. When he was out of sight, she ran to a strategic spot along the winding trail where the runners eventually would pass. Even though the runners were nowhere in sight, she continued to cheer, "GO, STU!"

"Pat, do you have to yell so loud?" my husband asked.

"Yep," she answered. "GO, STU!"

Steve inched his way a few paces behind us and pretended he had no idea who we were.

"GO, STU!"

I'll admit I was a little embarrassed, too. Pat had no shame.

At one point when she yelled, "GO, STU!" a man from across the park shouted, "HE CAN'T HEEEAAARRR YOOOUUU!"

"Pat, Stu can't hear you when he's deep in the woods. Why don't you let up a bit?" I asked.

"I don't know if he can hear me or not, but if he can, think how encouraged he'll be." So for sixteen minutes, this little dynamo continued to pump confidence and inspiration into her son's heart.

Later, I asked my nephew, "Stu, when you were running on that trail, could you hear your mother cheering for you?"

"Oh, yes," he answered. "I heard her the whole way."

"And what does that do for you?"

"It makes me not want to quit," he replied. "When my legs and lungs ache, when I feel like I'm going to throw up, I hear my mom cheering, and it makes me want to keep going."

A few years later, my son too became a cross-country runner, and I've learned a few facts about a footrace. As you near the end of the race, your throat burns, your legs ache, and your whole body cries out for you to stop. That's when friends and fans are the most valuable. Their encouragement helps you push through the pain to the finish.

A Cheerleader for Life

That's a beautiful picture of what a blessed mother can do for her children as they embark on the great race of life. The mother whose children rise up and call her blessed is an Encourager. Like Pat, her encouraging voice can be heard echoing in the distance, pumping courage and confidence into her children's hearts. She's the cheerleader on the sidelines who knows that an uplifting word, offered at the right moment, might make the difference between her children finishing well or collapsing along the way.

Webster defines *encouragement* as "to give courage or confidence to, to raise the hopes of, to help on by sympathetic advice and interest, to promote or stimulate." The primary way we encourage others is by the words we speak. William Barclay once said:

> One of the highest of human duties is the duty of encouragement. It is easy to laugh at men's ideas; it is easy to pour cold water on their enthusiasm; it is easy to discourage others. The world is full of discouragers. We have a Christian duty to encourage one another. Many a time a word of praise or thanks or appreciation or cheer has kept a man on his feet. Blessed is the man who speaks such a word.[1]

There's that word "blessed" again. Blessed is the mother who offers a word of praise, thanks, appreciation, or cheer to her children.

*T*he Power of a Word

The Bible has much to say about the power of our words. James compares the tongue to three relatively small entities that control something comparatively larger. First, he compares the tongue to a bit in a horse's mouth—a small piece of metal that steers a large animal to the left or the right or brings him to a halt. Second, James compares the tongue to a ship's rudder. And finally, he compares the tongue to a tiny spark that can start a forest fire.

Although James warns that our words can cause great destruction, they can also spark growth and motivation. James 3:6 states, "The tongue [the words we speak] . . . sets on fire the course of our life"(NASB). A mother's words have the power to change the direction of a child's life. What an awesome gift we can give!

One Sunday while visiting a church, author and speaker Florence Littauer was called on, without prior notice, to come forward and present the children's sermon. The following day Florence was to instruct the church staff on how to speak spontaneously, so she couldn't very well refuse this unscheduled "opportunity." As she walked to the front, she prayed for the Lord to lead her in what to say. The children filed out of the pews and followed her, their Pied Piper, down the aisle. As they clustered around her feet, Florence decided she would teach them a verse she had taught her now-grown children about the words we speak.

"Children, this morning I am going to teach you one verse that I taught my own children. Do you think you can learn one verse?" They nodded their heads.

"The verse is Ephesians 4:29, 'Let no corrupt communication proceed out of your mouth, but that which is good to the use of edifying, that it may minister grace unto the hearers.' Does anyone know what that means?" They shook their heads and looked at her as if she had just uttered Martian phrases.

So Florence and the children took the verse apart, word by word, and made some amazing discoveries. They surmised that we shouldn't say bad words to each other but good words. We should use our words to build up people, like stacking building blocks on top of one another, higher and higher. One little boy added that we should never knock anybody's blocks over. Our words should give grace, which is like giving a present. Finally, a little girl stood up, stepped into the aisle, and loudly stated to the congregation, "What she means is that our words should be like silver boxes with bows on top." The children had taught a lesson that the adults would not soon forget.[2]

As mothers, we may not be able to lavish name-brand clothes on our children, take them on exotic vacations, or fill their rooms with the latest electronic wonders. But we can give the gift more precious than any of these: the present of encouraging words. That gift is the spark that can start a fire burning in their hearts, spurring them on to accomplish great things.

Studies show that in the average home, ten negative comments are made for every positive one. Also, it takes four positive comments to counteract one negative statement. With that ratio, it's easy to understand why so many children are discouraged and have poor self-images.[3]

Changing the Course

A wise mother can speak a word that can change the course of a life, to her own children and to other children as well. Marion had such a mother. Marion was in first grade in 1942. She loved most everything about first grade: the smell of the chalk and color of the crayons; the way the old wooden floors smelled after the janitor had waxed them; having her own desk; and her teacher, Miss Edna. Marion decided that all angels must have blue eyes and smell like Jergen's Lotion because that was what Miss Edna looked and smelled like. The only thing Marion didn't like about first grade was Mildred.

Now, Mildred already had been to first grade one time, so she was bigger than everybody else. She didn't have any friends and seemed to concentrate on making enemies. Each day, as Marion walked home from school, Mildred would taunt her. Mildred would come up behind Marion and step on the backs of her shoes, causing them to slide down. Then, when Marion stopped to adjust them, Mildred would slap her hard on the back. Each day Marion dreaded the walk home.

Eventually, Marion's mother figured out something was wrong at school. Marion reluctantly told her mom about Mildred but begged her not to intervene, knowing that would only make matters worse.

The following day, Miss Edna asked Marion to stay after school to clean the erasers. Thinking that perhaps Mildred would be long gone by the time she walked home, Marion's heart leaped with joy (and appreciation). However, when Marion left school, her nemesis was waiting at the top of the hill.

Seeing Marion come home in tears once more, her wise mother came up with a plan. The following day she announced she would walk her daughter to school.

Marion was skeptical to say the least. Much later in life, she recounted the story this way:

> Why couldn't my mother understand that no plan she had dreamed up was going to work? We bundled up against the bitter cold and started walking up the hill. Maybe we wouldn't see Mildred, I hoped. But my mother had this confident look. I knew the look well, and I had a sinking feeling that we would see Mildred and that Mother would use her "plan."
>
> Sure enough, just as we reached the top of the hill and had to part company, I going in one direction and my mother in the opposite direction to her job at the bank, we spotted Mildred. We waited a few horrible moments as Mildred approached us. She pretended not to see us when she realized I had my mother with me.
>
> "Hello, Mildred," Mother said quietly. Mildred stopped, frozen as still

as a statue. Her hands and face were bright red from the intense cold. Her oversized coat hung open. There were only two buttons on it. The rest were missing. Underneath she wore a cotton dress, as though it were summer. I was wrapped up so snugly, I could hardly walk. I even had to wear under-shirts.

Mother stooped down to Mildred's level. She didn't say anything at first. Instead she rapidly buttoned Mildred's coat and turned up the collar around her neck. Then she fastened back this stubborn piece of hair that forever hung in Mildred's face. I stood off to one side watching our breath linger in front of our faces in the frigid morning air, praying that no students would happen by and that my mother's plan would be over quickly.

"I'm Marion's mother. I need your help, Mildred."

Mildred looked intently at my mother with an expression I couldn't identify. Their faces were inches apart. My mother's gloved hands held Mildred's cold ones as she spoke. "Marion doesn't have any brother or sisters. She sort of needs a special best friend at school. Someone to walk up the hill with her after school. You look like you'd be a fine friend for her. Would you be Marion's friend, Mildred?"

Mildred chewed on her bottom lip, blinking all the time, and then nodded.

"Oh, thank you!" Mama said with certain confidence and gratitude. "I just know you are someone I can depend on." Then she hugged Mildred long and hard. She gave me a quick hug and called to us as though nothing un-usual had happened, "'Bye, girls. Have a good day."[4]

You can guess the rest of the story. The two girls did become friends, best friends. As a matter of fact, Mildred starting having lots of friends. She started making good grades, and her desk wasn't so messy anymore. And she always wore her coat collar flipped up and that scraggly piece of hair pinned over to the side, just the way Marion's mom had fixed it.

Undoubtedly Mildred's building blocks had been knocked over many times, but Marion's mom gave her the gift of encouraging words. Marion's mom became Mildred's chief cheerleader, and that changed the course of a life.

A mother cheers for her child beginning the moment she holds her infant in her arms. She speaks sweetly to her new charge. With her eyes locked onto her child's, she silently speaks volumes to the treasure she has cradled to her breast, communicating, "You are special and very valuable to me."

The blessed mother cheers for the bundle of joy when the baby rolls over, laughs, and kicks her tiny feet into the air. She even gives a hurrah when the baby burps. (My, how things change from infancy to puberty!) She encourages the baby when he shakes a rattle, holds a cup, points to a color, and responds to his name. But mostly, she praises the child for no reason at all. "Just because you're mine."

If we leave our child's cheering section, if our seat is vacant, the child will look for someone else to fill it. That someone is usually a peer. So dust off those pom-poms! Ready that megaphone! Be about the business of becoming your child's greatest fan!

CHAPTER NINE

*C*heers
or Jeers

*E*very day we have a choice. Will we build up our children or tear them down? Are we their chief cheerleader or their chief critic? Do we encourage, uplift, inspire confidence, and give courage? Or do we discourage, condemn, and belittle?

I remember taking Steven to an amusement park to have a special mother-son day before he started fourth grade. Now, I detest amusement parks. They are hot. The lines are long. And the rides make me queasy. I was feeling quite the martyr as I made this personal sacrifice. I certainly hoped he appreciated what a great mom he had.

Being unsure that he had come to this realization, I thought I should bring it to his attention. We were poised at the top of the "Powder Keg Flume" ride, which was about to hurl us down a roller coaster track that ended in a pool of water intended to soak us. I leaned forward to Steven and was just about to say, "Steven, you are so lucky to have a mom like me to bring you to a place like this." But before the words came out of my mouth, the Holy Spirit stopped me. Was that what I wanted to say? Would those words build up Steven?

I leaned forward, wrapped my arms around my precious young son, and said, "Steven, I'm so lucky to have a son like you that I can bring to a place like this!"

With those words, a dimpled smile spread across his face, and I was thankful for the splash of the watery roller coaster that disguised the tears streaming down my face.

If I had spoken that first sentence, Steven wouldn't have felt lucky in the slightest to have a mom like me. He would have felt guilty and that he owed me something. However, the revised version made him feel special, treasured, and loved.

Now, who was encouraged? Actually, we both were.

Perhaps you have some old tapes from your past that you tend to replay with your children. Did your mother make comments that caused you to feel guilty or indebted to her for the care she gave you? Perhaps she still does. Many moms could be travel agents for guilt trips. Is that how you want to be remembered? It's never too late to change.

I had success with my words that day at the amusement park, but not every day has been a banner day. I've sometimes used my words to tear down instead of build up.

The tongue is a fire and the very world of iniquity, as James so aptly points out (3:6). It can only be tamed by the Holy Spirit's power. God has given those who are in Christ Jesus access to that power. The Spirit is referred to as our Helper (Romans 8:26). Just as a wild horse can be trained through hours and hours of discipline, so our tongue can be tamed by spending time with the Lord and through practice.

Lingering Echoes

Our words do more than just make our children feel good. Our words can make them feel like somebody who can accomplish great dreams— or like nobody, who is destined to be a loser.

As children, we learn many cute little sayings. "Early to bed, early to rise, makes a man healthy, wealthy, and wise." "Don't put all your eggs in one basket." "A stitch in time saves nine." But one adage I remember reciting as I was mercilessly teased by the neighborhood boys was, "Sticks and stones may break my bones, but words will never hurt me." Nothing could be further from the truth, for the pain of a hurtful word lingers long after the pain of a broken bone is forgotten. And when a mother utters the hurtful words, the effects can linger for a lifetime.

Bob, an acquaintance of mine, told me about how his mother's hurtful words had lingered for many years. When he was in his twenties, he worked in a family business with his father. Bob was diligent and won recognition for his work. He, his young bride, and his parents went to a banquet, where he was to accept his business award. He sat at the dinner table, anticipating hearing his name called from the podium. Then his mother leaned over and said, "You need to thank your father for this, Bob. You didn't really earn this award. Your father earned it for you."

Bob's mother stole her son's gift before he even held it in his hand. She had offered a jeer, not a cheer. Twenty years had passed when Bob told me this story, but the pain was etched on his face as though it had happened the day before.

Words will never hurt me? I don't think so.

Stories like Bob's cause me to pray the following poem, that I might use my tongue to bless rather than to hurt.

Silver Boxes

My words were harsh and hasty
And they came without a thought.
Then I saw the pain and anguish
That my bitter words had brought.

Bitter words that I had spoken
Made me think back through the past;
Of how many times I'd uttered
Biting words whose pain would last.

Then I wondered of the people
I had hurt by things I'd said;
All the ones I had discouraged
When I didn't use my head.

Then I thought about my own life,
Of painful words I've heard;
And of the times I'd been discouraged
By a sharp and cruel word.

And now clearly I remember
All the things I might have done;
But, by a word I was discouraged
And they never were begun.

Lord, help my words be silver boxes,
Neatly wrapped up with a bow;
That I give to all so freely,
As through each day I gladly go.

Silver boxes full of treasure,
Precious gifts from God above;
That all the people I encounter
Might have a box of God's own love.

—Michael Bright[1]

Florence Littauer says, "When it is a mother who steals our box, we can end up feeling like plain brown wrapping paper, looking for the glow of the silver for the rest of our lives."[2] Or as Proverbs expresses that thought, "An anxious heart weighs a man [or a child] down, but a kind word cheers him up" (Proverbs 12:25).

Your "Friend" Voice

Not only do our words have the power to bring discouragement, but our tone also is important. One day Susan, after ending a conversation with a telemarketer, was asked by her ten-year-old daughter, "Mom, that wasn't a friend, was it?"

"No," she replied. "How did you know that?"

"Because you weren't using your 'friend' voice."

What "voice" are we using with our children? Is it our "friend" voice or our "you're a bother" voice?

When Steven was fifteen, he had called a friend on the telephone. "Hello, may I speak to Tony?" he asked.

The mother on the other end gave out a heavy "you're bothering me" sigh and said, "OK. Hold on." Then she yelled out, "Tony, get the phone!"

Steven felt very uncomfortable. I'm sure his friend was embarrassed, but maybe not. Perhaps it was the norm at his house.

In any case, Mom, watch that tone. It can say more than the words themselves. But obviously the combination can be lethal or loving, as the following poem expresses.

> "I got two A's," the small boy said
> His voice was filled with glee.
> His father very bluntly asked,
> "Why didn't you get three?"
>
> "Mom, I've got the dishes done,"
> The girl called from the door.
> Her mother very calmly said,
> "Did you sweep the floor?"
>
> "I mowed the grass," the tall boy said,
> "And put the mower away."
> His father asked him with a shrug,
> "Did you clean off the clay?"
>
> The children in the house next door
> Seemed happy and content.
> The same things happened over there,
> But this is how it went.

"I got two A's," the small boy said
His voice was filled with glee.
His father proudly said, "That's great;
I'm glad you belong to me."

"Mom, I got the dishes done,"
The girl called fom the door.
Her mother smiled and softly said,
"Each day I love you more."

"I've mowed the grass," the tall boy said.
"And put the mower away."
His father answered with much joy,
"You've made my happy day."

Children deserve just simple praise
For tasks they're asked to do
If they're to lead a happy life,
So much depends on you!
　　　　　—Author Unknown

*W*hat Position Do You Play?

Some of the greatest sports fans are the parents of T-ball players. Steven started to play T-ball when he was five years old, and I found out that spectating T-ball was like watching a circus. Helmets that were too large balanced on tiny heads. Outfielders performed cartwheels and kicked the dirt to see who could make the biggest dust cloud. No one was sure what direction to run when—and if—the ball was hit. The coach, like a ringmaster with unruly performers, was forever flapping his arms, trying to get the boys to round the bases in the right order.

The softball was teed up on a pole, and the player's bat was supposed to connect with the ball. When it did, the crowd went wild! No one kept score (except maybe some of the more competitive parents, who tallied it in their heads). The boys played all positions, rotating with each inning.

Once Steven's grandfather asked, "What position do you play?" Steven just shrugged, not having a clue what "position" even meant—and skipped off happily to play with his friends. But after a few years of watching a child play the game, the coach figures out where the kid's talents lie. He then assigns him or her a position—a place where the coach feels the child will be a peak performer and benefit the team the most. So, too, a mother's goal is to discover her "players'" gifts and talents. Then she can steer them in the right direction and encourage them to develop their God-given potential. I admit it can be puzzling at times, and you can feel like a miner, hunting for that illusive gold. *Pam Farrell, Discovering the Hidden Treasure in Your Child*

A Mining Kind of Mother

Author and mother Lysa Terkeurst, in *The Best of the Proverbs 31 Ministry,* notes, "When a miner heads into the mine looking for gold, he has to move tons of dirt to get just a little gold. But he doesn't go in looking for dirt . . . he's looking for gold. Every child has little nuggets of gold inside just waiting to be discovered, but there may be lots of dirt that has to moved. Just remember, the more gold you look for, the more you will find."[3] And also remember, mining takes patience and persistence.

When your child experiences a success, applaud loudly, give a pat on the back, make it a banner day. Such affirmations build confidence and make a child want to do it again.

Businessman Charles Schwab said, "I have yet to find the man—however exalted his station—who did not do better work and put forth greater effort under a spirit of approval than under a spirit of criticism."[4] If I may be so bold as to modify Mr. Schwab, I have yet to find the child—however gifted or talented—who did not put forth greater effort in school, sports, or at home, under a spirit of approval rather than under a spirit of criticism.

How does the blessed mother go about discovering those hidden talents and gifts that she can encourage her child to pursue? She goes to the One who put them there in the first place. She is a Beacon, with her searchlight watching over her fleet. She is listening to her child's interests and dreams. She prays and pays attention.

My husband found out just how quietly determined such a mother can be when he walked up to one of our neighbors, the mom of a strapping 6-foot, 2-inch, 210-pound young man and said, "That boy ought to be playing football."

The boy's mother smiled and said, "He plays cello." She understood her son's gift and talents and proudly supported him.

Accentuate the Positive

Many moms (myself included) tend to try to strengthen the child's weakness to the detriment of the strengths. When I find myself putting the emphasis in the wrong place, I recall this story.

A group of animals decided to improve their general welfare by starting a school. The curriculum included swimming, running, climbing, and flying. The duck, an excellent swimmer, was deficient in other areas, so he majored in climbing and flying, much to the detriment of his swimming. The rabbit, a superior runner, was forced to spend so much time in other classes that he soon lost much of his famed speed. The squirrel, who had been rated A as a climber, dropped to a C because his instructors spent hours trying to teach him to fly. And the eagle could no longer soar to the treetops because he had to learn how to swim.[5]

Although we can't ignore our children's weaknesses, we can focus on their strengths. Steven is gifted in math and science. However, foreign languages are a struggle. Does that mean I allow him to ignore Spanish assignments and approach the subject with a flippant attitude? No, but I'm not going to encourage him to become a Spanish major, either.

Steven is a very creative writer. However, his spelling is also very creative. Suppose he handed me a story to read, but instead of cheering him on and praising his creative ability, I pulled out a red marker and pointed out all his spelling errors? What would that do to his love of writing? I suspect it would quench it.

Please understand that negative words are sometimes spoken in my home. As mothers, part of our job is to reprimand, scold, correct, and punish. Proverbs says, "He who spares the rod hates his son, but he who loves him is careful to discipline him" (Proverbs 13:24). Let's just say, Steven has definitely been loved.

Sometimes encouragement doesn't come in the form of a pat on the back but on an extremity several inches south of there. As one writer said, "We ought to employ the carrot more than the stick, but the stick has its uses."[6]

Do you remember that old song from the '40s that talked about accentuating the positive and eliminating the negative? Though a mother can't afford to turn a blind eye to negative behavior and detrimental character flaws, she can make it her mission to discover her child's special gifts and talents. Once she's caught a glimpse of those abilities, she can become the child's biggest cheerleader and encourage him to develop what he's good at.

CHAPTER TEN

*Y*ou Win Some, You Lose Some

*G*reat fans have been called the sixth player on a basketball court. What a difference their support and encouragement can make. That's why every team going into the play-offs hopes for home court advantage. It's much easier to face a crowd that's cheering than a crowd that's hurling insults and jeers.

During the day, our children face cutting remarks from peers, rejection on the playground, and insecurities because of cliques. When they walk through the front door, they need to know they are safe and that they now have home court advantage.

Fair-weather fans tend to reject their hero when he doesn't perform up to expectations. They leave the game early if their team is behind. Genuine fans remain devoted even when their team faces defeat and failure. They stay around until the bitter end. When our children face failure and discouragement, we must dust them off and send them back out there to try again.

What makes one person quit after a failure while others press on? I believe a family can create an environment that allows children to fail and then to move ahead. If your child never fails, you could be overprotective, or your child could be playing it too safe. If we aren't a little nervous about our attempts in life, then we're probably not living up to our potential. That's true for adults as well as children. Theodore Roosevelt said, "The only man who never makes a mistake is the man who never does anything."[1]

Countering "I Can't"

Creating a positive attitude in some children can be quite a laborious task. My son was born with a propensity to quit if his efforts didn't meet with success on the first try. He would throw down his blocks and declare, "I can't do it!" When we were trying to teach him to ride his bicycle without the training wheels, he fell several times. Then came his take on the situation, "I can't do this!"

"Steven," I said, "you can't do it *yet*. But you will do it eventually, if you keep trying. One day, riding your bike will be the funnest thing you'll do as a boy."

He placed his chubby hands on his hips, looked me square in the eye, and said, "This is not fun. This will never be fun. And I can't do it!"

I could have said, "Just forget it! You're a quitter." But I persisted.

A few days later, he hopped on his little red bike and rode and rode and rode. And guess what? It *was* fun!

Did I get tired of cheerleading during all those "I can't, I quit, and I'll never get it" days? Yup! Did I lay down my pom-poms and march off the field? Nope.

We finally had to outlaw the words "I can't" in our household. "Can't" was placed in the category with other four-letter words. We've stressed that failure is an event, not a person.

To further encourage Steven, I bought him a T-shirt that across the back read, "Quitting is not an option," which he wore until it was threadbare. I also placed the following poem in his room as a reminder of our "I can't" rule.

The Man Who Thinks He Can

If you think you are beaten, you are.
If you think you dare not, you don't.

If you like to win, but think you can't,
It's almost a cinch you won't.
If you think you'll lose, you're lost,
For out in the world we find
Success begins with a fellow's will.
It's all in the state of mind.

If you think you're outclassed, you are.
You've got to think high to rise.
You've got to be sure of yourself before
You can ever win a prize.
Life's battles don't always go
To the stronger or faster man,
But sooner or later, the man who wins
Is the man who thinks he can.

—Author Unknown[2]

These facts will encourage your "I can't" child—and you:

- After Fred Astaire's first screen test in 1933, the director noted, "Can't act! Slightly bald. Can dance a little."
- Louisa May Alcott, author of *Little Women,* was encouraged to find work as a servant or a seamstress.
- Beethoven's violin teacher once told him he was a "hopeless composer."
- Walt Disney was fired by a newspaper editor for lack of ideas.
- Thomas Edison's teacher said he was too stupid to learn anything.
- Albert Einstein didn't speak until he was four years old and didn't read until he was seven. His teachers described him as mentally slow.
- Isaac Newton did poorly in grade school.
- Henry Ford failed and went bankrupt five times before he finally succeeded.
- Babe Ruth set the home run record (714), but he also held the record for the most strikeouts (1,330).

- Winston Churchill failed sixth grade.
- One basketball player missed 9,000 shots in his career. He lost more than 300 games. Twenty-six times he was trusted to take the game's winning shot and missed. His name is Michael Jordan. He said, "I've failed over and over again in my life. And that's why I succeed."[3]

A Season for Everything

Although we all want to be encouraging moms, when a child is in the throes of emotional upheaval because of failure, don't respond by being the bouncing cheerleader who tries to cheer him or her up. First, follow the advice of Romans 12:15, "Rejoice with those who rejoice, and weep with those who weep" (NASB).

In the seventh grade, Steven was cut from the school basketball team. In his eyes, he was a failure. Instead of weeping with those who weep, I tried to be Susie Cheerleader. "Oh, that's OK. Did you know that Michael Jordan was cut from his high school basketball team?"

Steven jeered at me and said through his teeth, "It's not OK, and if I hear one more word about Michael Jordan being cut, I'm going to get sick!" Apparently, his coach had offered the same consolation!

Remember when you faced a loss and your well-meaning friends tried to cheer you up? But all you wanted was for someone to hold you and say, "I'm so sorry."

I remember going through years of infertility and the loss of a child a few months after conception. To me, that was failure. I heard comments such as "All things work together for good" and "At least you have one child." These words didn't encourage me at that tender moment.

Like you, your child needs understanding and support when facing a failure. Allow an appropriate time to pass before spurring him on to try again.

But try again he must. Failure is the price of excellence. We all win some. We all lose some. But if we can teach our children that to win is to rise each time we fall, then we will have taught the lesson that turns children into champions.

One of my favorite poems is about a race. In these verses, I see myself as the runner and my heavenly Father's voice encouraging me on. Envision yourself in these words, and then use them to encourage your children as they run the great race of life.

The Race

I

"Quit! Give up! You're beaten!"
        They shout at me and plead.
"There's just too much against you now.
        This time you can't succeed."

And as I start to hang my head
        In front of failure's face
My downward fall is broken by
        The memory of a race.

And hope refills my weakened will
        As I recall that scene;
For just the thought of that short race
        Rejuvenates my being.

II

A children's race—young boys, young men—
        How I remember well.
Excitement, sure! But also fear;
        It wasn't hard to tell.

They all lined up so full of hope;
        Each thought to win that race.
Or tie for first, or if not that,
        At least take second place.

And fathers watched from off the side
    Each cheering for his son.
And each boy hoped to show his dad
    That he would be the one.

The whistle blew and off they ran
    Young hearts and hopes afire.
To win and be the hero there
    Was each young boy's desire.

And one boy in particular,
    Whose dad was in the crowd,
Was running near the lead and thought:
    "My dad will be so proud!"

But as they speeded down the field
    Across a shallow dip,
The little boy who thought to win
    Lost his step and slipped.

Trying hard to catch himself,
    His hands flew out to brace,
And mid the laughter of the crowd
    He fell flat on his face.

So down he fell and with him hope
    —He couldn't win it now—
Embarrassed, sad, he only wished
    To disappear somehow.

But as he fell his dad stood up
    And showed his anxious face,
Which to the boy so clearly said:
    "Get up and win the race."

He quickly rose, no damage done
    —Behind a bit, that's all—
And ran with all his mind and might
    To make up for the fall.

So anxious to restore himself
    —To catch up and to win—
His mind went faster than his legs:
    He slipped and fell again!

He wished then he had quit before
    With only one disgrace.
"I'm hopeless as a runner now;
    I shouldn't try to race."

But in the laughing crowd he searched
    And found his father's face;
That steady look, which said again:
    "Get up and win the race!"

So up he jumped to try again
    —Ten yards behind the last—
"If I'm to gain those yards," he thought,
    "I've got to move real fast."

Exerting everything he had
    He regained eight or ten,
But trying so hard to catch the lead
    He slipped and fell again!

Defeat! He lay there silently
    —A tear dropped from his eye—
"There's no sense running anymore;
    Three strikes: I'm out! Why try!"

The will to rise had disappeared;
    All hope had fled away;
So far behind, so error prone;
    A loser all the way.

"I've lost, so what's the use?" he thought.
    "I'll live with my disgrace."
But then he thought about his dad,
    Who soon he'd have to face.

"Get up," an echo sounded low.
    "Get up and take your place;
You were not meant for failure here.
    Get up and win the race."

"With borrowed will get up," it said,
    "you haven't lost at all.
For winning is no more than this:
    To rise each time you fall."

So up he rose to run once more,
And with a new commit
He resolved that win or lose
At least he wouldn't quit.

So far behind the others now,
—The most he'd ever been—
Still he gave it all he had
And ran as though to win.

Three times he'd fallen, stumbling;
Three times he rose again;
Too far behind to hope to win,
He still ran to the end.

They cheered the winning runner
As he crossed the line first place.
Head high, and proud, and happy;
No falling, no disgrace.

But when the fallen youngster
Crossed the line last place,
The crowd gave him the greater cheer
For finishing the race.

And even though he came in last
With head bowed low, unproud,
You would have thought he'd won the race
To listen to the crowd.

And to his dad he sadly said,
 "I didn't do well."
"To me, you won," his father said.
 "You rose each time you fell."

III

And now when things seem dark and hard
 And difficult to face,
The memory of that little boy
 Helps me in my race.

For all of life is like that race,
 With ups and downs and all.
And all you have to do to win,
 Is rise each time you fall.

"Quit! Give up! You're beaten!"
 They still shout in my face.
But another voice within me says:
 "GET UP AND WIN THE RACE!"

  — D. H. (Dee) Groberg
   Used by permission of the author

The Bible is packed with "cheerleaders." Elizabeth encouraged Mary; the widow encouraged Elijah; Ruth encouraged Naomi; Barnabas encouraged Mark. But perhaps one of the best cheerleaders was Paul, writer of more than half the New Testament. Now, I know it might be hard to visualize tough and rugged Paul with pom-poms and a megaphone, but those pleated skirts were quite the rage in Rome!

In each of his letters to the various churches, Paul began with encouraging words. "I . . . do not cease giving thanks for you" (Ephesians 1:15–16 NASB). "I thank my God in all my remembrance of you, always offering prayer with joy . . . for you all" (Philippians 1:3–4 NASB). "I have you in my heart" (Philippians 1:7 NASB). "We give thanks to God, the Father of our Lord Jesus Christ, praying always for you" (Colossians 1:3 NASB). "Kindle afresh the gift of God which is in you" (2 Timothy 1:6 NASB).

Even though Paul's letters were sprinkled with encouraging words, their primary purpose was to exhort, instruct, and, yes, correct. His corrections were stern. ("Stop gossiping." "Quit sinning." "Stop going over the elementary principles and move on to the meat of the Word." "You foolish Galatians, who has bewitched you!" "I fear for you that perhaps I have labored in vain.") No, Paul was never known as a pushover, but his reproofs were wrapped in love.

Paul was an encourager to his son in the Lord, Timothy, telling Timothy that he believed in him. Not only that, Paul gave Timothy great responsibility and reassured the youth of his confidence that he could do the job.

Timothy was a young man when Paul sent him to resolve several serious problems in the church at Ephesus. No doubt Paul's words of encouragement built confidence in the lad. "Don't let anyone look down on you because you are young, but set an example for the believers in speech, in life, in love, in faith and in purity" (1 Timothy 4:12). Sure, Paul could have sent someone older and more mature. Instead he sent Timothy and assured him that Paul trusted him and that he could handle the job. All the while, Paul was on the sidelines cheering, "GO, TIMOTHY! You can do it!" And Timothy did.

If ever there was an encourager, it was God Himself. And it is interesting that some of His most encouraging messages were addressed to teenagers. For example, he spoke to the young Jeremiah and appointed him to be a prophet to the nations. Jeremiah questioned God's call, but God reassured him that He would give him the words and the power to succeed. He said, "Before I formed you in the womb I knew you, and before you were born I consecrated you." Jeremiah argued that he was but a youth, but God, the Encourager, said, "Do not say, 'I am a youth,' because everywhere I send you, you shall go, and all that I command you, you shall speak. Do not be afraid of them, for I am with you to deliver you" (Jeremiah 1:5, 7–8 NASB).

Approximately 365 times in the Bible, God tells His people not to be afraid, and many of those persons were teens. In the Old Testament, God gave Joseph the courage to interpret the king's dreams. When King Darius issued a decree forbidding worshiping anyone but himself, God gave Daniel courage to continue worshiping Him, despite the threat of being thrown into a lions' den. The Lord gave Shadrach, Meshach, and Abednego courage to resist bowing down to King Nebuchadnezzar's false god, even if it meant being thrown into the fiery furnace. He gave David courage to fight the Philistine giant Goliath with a sling and a few rocks. He gave Mary courage to bear His Son, sending an angel to reassure her of her great call.

We can learn from the Master how to speak encouraging words to our children, but, most important, we need to teach our sons and daughters that true and lasting courage comes from Christ and being dependent on the Holy Spirit's power. The key to accomplishing great feats for God is found in Philippians 4:13: "I can do everything through Him who gives me strength."

- Good job!
- I'm glad you're my son (daughter).
- I like you!
- That was really great!
- I love the way you fixed your hair.
- That shirt looks great on you.
- You played that song beautifully.
- You're a great friend!
- You'll make a wonderful wife (husband) some day.
- Thanks for cleaning your room.
- You're so strong!
- I can always count on you.
- I trust you.
- You're God's special gift to me.
- You light up my day.
- My favorite part of the day is picking you up from school.
- I missed having you around today.
- You're such a good helper.
- I'm proud of you!
- Way to go! I knew you could do it!
- God made a masterpiece when He made you.
- You're such a treasure.
- You're one of God's greatest gifts to me.
- I'm behind you.
- I'm praying for you.
- That was so responsible.
- You're a joy.
- How did you get so smart!
- That was so creative.
- Hurray for you!
- Thank you.

CHAPTER ELEVEN

Catherine Carmichael: An Encouraging Mother

*F*or fifty-three years Amy Carmichael lived as a missionary in India, ministering to countless adults and children and telling of Jesus Christ's love. She began the Dohnavur Fellowship, a ministry for children rescued from the abuse of Hindu temple worship. During her lifetime, approximately 1,000 children were rescued, educated, nurtured, and introduced to Christ. Although Amy never married, she was blessed with hundreds of children who called her "Amma"—Mother. Her ministry, which took place in the 1800s and early 1900s, still lives on today.

How did one woman have such an impact on the world in a time when independent women were frowned upon? How did she have the courage to follow her dream to serve God in places where few dared to go? The answer lies in a mother who encouraged her children to heed God's call on their lives, no matter where that call led.

Catherine Carmichael and her husband, David, brought seven children into their happy little world of Millisle, Ireland, including Amy in 1867. The Carmichaels enjoyed a comfortable lifestyle, but Catherine wasn't afraid to hand out discipline when needed and then wrap that discipline in warm and loving arms. She provided discipline "balanced by buttered toast and raspberry jam in front of the nursery fire."[1]

Amy first learned about God's love and the power of prayer at her mother's knee. Catherine once told her, "Ask God, Amy, if you want anything badly. Share it with Him. He's never too far away to hear our prayers, and He'll always give you an answer."[2]

When Amy was three years old, she took her mother at her word. One thing she wanted more than anything else was to have big blue eyes like her mother's. So she prayed and asked God to change her brown eyes to match her mother's. The next day, she climbed up to look in the mirror, fully expecting to see blue eyes in her reflection. Instead, her brown eyes stared back at her.

Amy learned a valuable lesson. God always answers prayers. But sometimes He answers no.

When Amy's mother made soup for the sick and poor in the community, often she sent her children to deliver it. This was Amy's introduction to reaching out to the poor. She also loved to hear stories of India that her pastor's brother, Mr. Beatty, would tell. She couldn't learn enough about how the Lord worked in the hearts of the Indian people who had never heard about Jesus before.

As a seventeen-year-old, Amy began to teach little children in Belfast wherever she could gather them in a group. She also started a girls' prayer meeting and a boys' Bible study. On Sundays she held a class for girls who worked in the mills. These young girls were called "Shawlies" because they were so poor they couldn't afford to buy the hats they were expected to wear to church and wore shawls to cover their heads. Amy had to travel through dark alleys and through parts of town where drunken men roamed the streets. Belfast's sin-filled back streets made her heart ache, and she prayed for God to reach down and save these young girls out of the pit in which they lived.

Amy's ministry with the Shawlies grew to the point they needed a large building for the meetings. God provided such a place, and the girls named it "The Welcome," for all who needed physical and spiritual help were welcomed there. A few years later, Amy started a similar mission in England.

When she gathered children from the slums to teach them about God, her mother opened her home and even provided tea for refreshments. When Catherine's friends whispered behind her back, saying it was improper for Amy to travel into the slums and invite the Shawlies to her church, Catherine turned a deaf ear and praised her daughter's giving heart.

And when on January 13, 1892, Amy heard God's call to go to India, where she would spend the rest of her life, her mother gave Amy her blessing. Catherine Carmichael wasn't one to discourage her daughter from heeding God's call but instead encouraged her in both word and deed to do as God directed. She was a mother who trained up her child in the way she should go—and then let her go. She was an encourager who poured courage and confidence into her child by pointing her to the One who gives us strength.

When Amy wrote to her mother about going away to India, Catherine responded with the following letter.

> Yes, dearest Amy, He has lent you to me all these years. He only knows what a strength, comfort and joy you have been to me. In sorrow He made you my staff and solace, in loneliness my more than child companion, and now in my gladness my bright and merry-hearted sympathizer. So, darling, when He asks you now to go away from within my reach, can I say nay? No, no, Amy, He is yours—you are His—to take you where He pleases and to use you as He pleases. I can trust you to Him and I do. . . . All day He has helped me, and my heart unfailingly says, Go ye.[3]

How did Amy rise up and call her mother blessed? She wrote, "There never was such a mother so good, so loving, so unselfish, so perfect in every way. We can only thank God for her and try to make her shadowed life bright with our love."[4]

Some have had kings in their lineage,
Some to whom honor was paid.
I don't have those as my ancestors
But I have a mother who prays.
I have a mother who prays for me

And pleads with the Lord every day for me.
Oh what a difference it makes for me
I have a mother who prays.
My mother's prayers cannot save me,
Only mine can avail;
But Mother introduced me to someone,
someone who never could fail.
Oh yes . . . I have a mother who prays for me
And pleads with the Lord every day for me.
O what a difference it makes for me
I have a mother who prays.

—Author unknown[5]

For the mother is and must be, whether she knows it or not, the greatest, strongest, and most lasting teacher her children have.

—Hannah Whitall Smith

My mother had a great deal of trouble with me, but I think she enjoyed it.

—Mark Twain

SECTION FOUR

Be a
Self-Esteem
Builder

CHAPTER TWELVE

*J*oining the Construction Crew

*W*henever I walk into a lumberyard, my mind races back to my childhood days of playing in the warehouse of my daddy's lumber company in Rocky Mount, North Carolina. I still can smell the freshly cut timbers in the mill-work shop and see the mounds of sawdust piled under imposing band saws.

I recall hours of talking with the shop's old-timers who made raised panels for doors and cabinets. Since none of the men had all their fingers, I was convinced I needed to steer clear of the powerful saws.

On Saturdays, I'd ride around town with my dad while he inspected various construction sites. I loved to run up and down skeleton stairwells in partially built homes but disliked it when he spent what seemed like hours inspecting new construction where only the foundation was complete.

"Sharon," he would say, "the foundation is the most important part of a house. If the foundation isn't built just right, the walls can shift later, jeopardizing the integrity of the entire structure."

I also learned that two builders can work from the same blueprint but end up with very different products. The difference between an average home and a superbly built home is in the quality of materials and the attention to detail.

As mothers, we all have access to the same blueprint to build godly children: the Scriptures. But the end result may depend on the quality of mothering we provide and our attention to detail.

The writer of Proverbs refers to mothers as builders when he says, "The wise woman builds her house, but the foolish tears it down with her own hands" (Proverbs 14:1 NASB). We have the chance to be a part of God's construction crew or Satan's wrecking crew.

In the last section, we looked at the blessed mother who is an encourager. Kissing cousin to giving the gift of encouragement is building self-esteem. What we build into our children's hearts serves as their foundation as they encounter a lifetime of victories and defeats.

Confidence in Christ

Self-esteem is how a person feels about himself, how much he likes the person that he is, how comfortable he is with his weaknesses, and how in tune to his strengths. Is that biblical? Absolutely. A proper understanding of who we are in Christ gives great confidence. This understanding also keeps us from becoming prideful, as we realize nothing we have done or ever could do enables us to attain such a heavenly inheritance. Jesus did it for us. We have great worth, not because of *who* we are but because of *whose* we are, and that keeps self-esteem in perspective.

True self-esteem isn't conceit. Someone with high proper self-esteem is so comfortable with who he is and the value he has as a child created in God's image that he has no need to try to impress others. Self-esteem based on appearance and performance is a false god and does result in pride.

Young David in the Bible is a wonderful example of a person who found his value in being a child of God. In 1 Samuel 17, David, who was probably a young teenager at the time, went to the battlefield where the Israelite and Philistine armies were at a standoff. David's task was to take provisions to his brothers. When he arrived, he saw how afraid the soldiers were of Goliath, a giant on the opposing side. He asked the men, "Who is this uncircumcised Philistine, that he should taunt the armies of the living God?" (verse 26 NASB). In other words, who does this guy think he is?

David didn't ask that question because he was conceited or because he was trying to impress anyone. But, because he knew God could work through him, he fought the giant when no one else was willing. David said, "The Lord who delivered me from the paw of the lion and from the paw of the bear, He will deliver me from the hand of this Philistine" (verse 37 NASB). And God did.

A child's self-esteem is especially susceptible to challenge during adolescence. Tony Campolo saw firsthand how our worth in Christ can give confidence when he served as a counselor in a junior high camp.

He soon found that a junior high kid's concept of a good time was to pick on people. In this particular case, at this particular camp, a boy suffered from cerebral palsy. His name was Billy. And the other boys picked on him. As the kids watched him pull his uncoordinated body across the campgrounds, they lined up and imitated his grotesque movements.

Tony watched Billy one day as he was asking for direction. "Which . . . way . . . is . . . the . . . craft . . . shop?" he stammered, his mouth contorting.

The boys mimicked, "It's . . . over . . . there . . . Billy." And then they laughed.

Tony was irate. But his furor reached its highest pitch when, on Thursday morning, the guys in Billy's cabin elected one of their own to give devotions to the whole group. Tony wondered what would happen, because the boys had appointed Billy to be the speaker. Tony knew they just wanted to get Billy up front to make fun of him.

As he dragged his way to the podium, giggles rolled over the crowd. It took Billy almost five minutes to say seven words: "Jesus . . . loves . . . me . . . and . . . I . . . love . . . Jesus."

When he finished, there was dead silence. Tony looked over his shoulder and saw junior high boys bawling all over the place. A revival broke out in that camp after Billy's short testimony. And now, as Tony Campolo travels all over the world, he finds missionaries and preachers who say, "Remember me? I was converted at that junior high camp."

"The counselors had tried everything to get those kids interested in Jesus," Tony recalls. "They even imported baseball players whose batting averages had gone up since they had started praying. But God chose not to use the superstars. He chose a kid with cerebral palsy to break the spirits of the haughty. He's that kind of God."[1]

Billy had learned an important lesson. His worth wasn't based on how well he could talk or walk. It wasn't based on appearance or intelligence. His worth was based on a simple truth: "Jesus loves me."

Dorothy Biggs wrote in her book *Your Child's Self-Esteem,*

> Your child's judgment of himself influences the kinds of friends he choos-
> es, how he gets along with others, the kind of person he marries, and how
> productive he will be. It affects his creativity, integrity, stability, and even
> whether he will be a leader or a follower. His feelings of self-worth form
> the core of his personality and determine the use he makes of his aptitudes
> and abilities. His attitude toward himself has direct bearing on how he lives
> all parts of his life. In fact, self-esteem is the mainspring that slates every child
> for success or failure as a human being.[2]

Self-esteem isn't built overnight. We instill a sense of esteem. I love
that word *instill.* It means to deposit a little at a time, drop by drop.
Through consistent deposits of unconditional love and acceptance, the
blessed mother makes the child feel valued and capable and imparts a sense
of belonging. A mother places the insulation of affection around her child
so he can withstand the external forces that desire to break down his
sense of himself and his God-given treasures.

Proverbs provides several insights into the necessary materials to
"build" our homes. No, Solomon isn't talking about bricks and mortar
or hammer and nails. He's not even talking about carpet swatches and col-
or schemes. "By *wisdom* a house is built, and through *understanding* it is
established; through *knowledge* its rooms are filled with rare and beautiful treasures" (24:3–4, italics added).

Remember, the difference between an average house and a superbly
built house is the quality of materials and the attention to detail. With
wisdom, understanding, and knowledge, you can't go wrong.

Don't you just love shopping by catalog? You simply pick up the phone
and speak to the operator. No crowded malls. No long checkout lines. No
hunting for a parking space. I have great news for you as you look over your
shopping list for materials that build self-esteem in your child. You can ac-
quire what you need directly from the Manufacturer. Pull out the catalog (the
Bible) and give Him a call. You'll never be disappointed with the quality,
and you'll be surprised at the unexpected bonuses that come with each request. "If any of you lacks wisdom, he should ask God, who gives generously to all without finding fault, and it will be given to him" (James 1:5).

So, moms, let's put on those hard hats and get to work!

CHAPTER THIRTEEN

The Foundation: Unconditional Love and Acceptance

*B*randon was raised in a family that didn't know how to show love. His parents never really got along and didn't try to hide their contempt for each other from the children. His mother worked full-time, and his father was an executive who rarely came home for dinner. Most days after school, Brandon let himself in the house with a key hidden in the mailbox and watched TV until his mom came home to cook dinner. Dinnertime was never pleasant. The family bickered or simply watched TV in silence. After the meal, Brandon spent his evenings alone in his room, listening to music or doing his homework.

Nobody at school knew how lonely Brandon felt. He was handsome, intelligent, charming, and even appeared cocky. He put on a superb act of having it all together, but on the inside he was dying for his parents' approval, acceptance, and unconditional love. All Brandon wanted was for someone to ask him how his day went, to notice when he did well, or to show it mattered if life wasn't so good for him.

As a teenager, Brandon drank heavily to numb the pain, but his parents barely noticed. One of his goals in life was to see how many girls he could coax into bed. There were many. As an adult, Brandon was still looking for love in all the wrong places.

The foundation for building self-esteem in your child is unconditional love and acceptance. That means affirming the child for who he is, not for what he does. And it means loving the child no matter what.

Even if he has a temper tantrum in the middle of a church service? No matter what. Even if she receives an F in math? No matter what. Even if he gets caught lying? No matter what. Even if she becomes pregnant? No matter what.

That doesn't mean we always like the behavior, but we always must love the child.

How to Love Like God

Unconditional love isn't easy. Only God loves perfectly. But the more time we spend with Him, the more we experience His unconditional love in our lives. And the more we allow Him to give us wisdom, understanding, and knowledge, then the more we will resemble Him and love as He loves.

Dr. Ross Campbell says he reminds himself of several foundational points when he is having trouble loving his children unconditionally. First, he recalls that they are children.

Second, much of childish behavior is unpleasant.

Third, if we do our part as parents and love our children despite their childish behavior, they will mature and give up childish ways.

Fourth, if we love them only when they please us (which is conditional love), and if we convey our love to them only during those times, they won't feel genuinely loved. This will make them feel insecure and actually prevent their moving into better self-control and more mature behavior. Therefore, their development and behavior are as much a parent's responsibility as it is theirs.

Fifth, if we love them only when they meet our requirements or expectations, they will feel incompetent and will believe it's pointless to do their best, since that's never enough. They will always be plagued by insecurity, anxiety, low self-esteem, and anger. To guard against this, a parent needs to remind herself often of her responsibility for their total growth.

Sixth, if we love them unconditionally, they will feel comfortable about themselves and will be able to control their anxiety and their behavior as they grow to adulthood.

Seventh, for our sake as struggling parents and for our sons' and daughters' sakes, pray that our love for our children will be as unconditional as we can make it. The future of our children depends on this foundation.[1]

The number one cause of poor self-esteem is the absence of unconditional love. Unfortunately, a parent's natural tendency is to love a child *if . . .* if she cleans her room, if she makes good grades, if she obeys quickly, if she has an acceptable appearance. Yet our goal is to love *despite . . .* despite the disappointing grades, despite the ignoring of our rules, despite our own impatience and imperfection.

*T*wo False Gods

Building strong self-esteem is quite a project, and it's complicated by two false gods that skew a person's self-perceived value: performance and appearance. The world teaches that a person will be loved and accepted if he performs well or if he is attractive.

Little girls grow up with Barbie as their standard. Yet, if you blew Barbie up to life-size proportions, she would measure in at 39–18–34 and be six feet tall. Now, how many of your friends fit that description? Barbie's only blemish is "Made in Japan" stamped on the bottom of her foot.

As I prepared to teach a seminar called "Unshakable Confidence in Christ," I went to buy a Barbie to use as a visual aid. Having been around mostly boys for the past sixteen years, I was amazed at all this little lady had accomplished. She has played in the WNBA, gone to dental school, become a veterinarian, starred in *Star Trek,* conquered bucking broncos, danced in the ballet, taught school, marched for animal rights, baby-sat, mastered shopping, starred in *Baywatch,* and become a pediatrician, just to name a few. Not only that, but she drives a sports car, has incredible hair, dates a handsome guy, and runs around with "beautiful" people.

All I wanted to do was buy a Barbie, but I got much more. I received an insight into why little girls grow up feeling as if they just don't measure up.

This isn't about bashing Barbie. Beauty, "the gold coin of human worth," as Dr. James Dobson calls it,[2] is paid homage in magazines, on TV, and even at the school playground.

Perhaps we need to examine the attitudes in our own homes. On what do we base a person's value: beauty, bank account, sports ability, intelligence, social status? Our homes are bugged, you know. Little ears are listening to what we say, and little persons are forming their own standards to live by.

What about little boys? What pressures do they feel from society? It's certainly not to be Barbie's friend Ken. I think theirs falls under the category of what society heralds as manly. James Bond could be considered the embodiment of an acceptable male: fast cars, fast women, indestructible body (bounces back after being run over by a train, falling from an airplane, and jumping from a twenty-story building), never gets hit by a barrage of bullets while never missing his target, makes a ton of money, loves his job, has lots of toys, and women clamor for his attention. That's a tall order to fill, yet society conveys the message that this is how a boy can gain acceptance and love.

If appearance and performance were the keys to self-esteem, then King Solomon should have been the happiest man who ever lived. He had power, position, possessions, and women (seven hundred wives and three hundred concubines!). Yet God granted him an extra measure of wisdom with which Solomon evaluated his accomplishments and his accumulated wealth. What was his take on his life? "Meaningless! Meaningless! . . . Utterly meaningless! Everything is meaningless" (Ecclesiastes 1:2). Status plus stuff doesn't equate personal wholeness and happiness.

How many mothers have propped the ladder of self-esteem against the wall and stood at the bottom to watch their children climb the rungs, only to find the ladder was leaning against the wrong wall?

The sad repercussion of such choices came home to me when my husband, who is a dentist, told me of a new patient he had examined recently. She was a beautiful girl who had been a cheerleader at a large state university. She seemed to have everything going for her—until she opened her mouth. When she did, he saw that her teeth were eroded to the gum line by stomach acids due to throwing up. She was bulimic. Her ladder had been leaning against the wrong wall, and when she reached the top, nothing was there.

Little girls don't grow up to be Barbie, and little boys don't grow up to be James Bond. If kids are left thinking that performance and appearance are the measure of a person's worth, they will lead lives of senseless striving that bring them nothing but frustration and depression. From the high chair to high school, they need to know that they are loved and accepted because each of them is a unique child of God, created in His image.

The false gods of performance and appearance have been around since the beginning of time. When the prophet Samuel went to the home of Jesse to appoint the next king of Israel, he was drawn to Jesse's son Eliab because of his height and appearance. But God chose Eliab's little brother David instead.

What was God's criterion? "The Lord does not look at the things man looks at. Man looks at the outward appearance, but the Lord looks at the heart" (1 Samuel 16:7).

The heart of the matter is the matter of the heart. When we love our children unconditionally, we love them just because they are ours. It's amazing how much confidence can be pumped into a child who knows he is loved and accepted no matter what.

"Magic" Formula

A study was conducted on two hundred boys from the Baltimore slums to predict their future success. Each boy's evaluation was the same: "He hasn't got a chance." Twenty-five years later, a follow-up study was done on the same boys. Of the 180 men located, 176 were successful lawyers, doctors, or businessmen. When asked to what they attributed their success, each mentioned a particular teacher's name.

The teacher was still alive, so the researchers sought her out and asked the old but alert lady what magic formula she had used to pull these boys from the slums into successful achievement. The teacher's eyes sparkled, and her lips broke into a gentle smile. "It's really very simple. I loved those boys."[3]

Love. That was her magic formula.

While children need to know that our love isn't based on appearance and performance, we need to reassure our kids in both of those areas. Girls want to know that they are pretty. Boys want to know that they are manly. This is especially true during those adolescent years when the boy is metamorphosing from a pudgy, pug-nosed kid into a fuzzy, lanky teen, and when that rectangular-shaped little girl with pigtails and ribbons changes into a curvy figure who wears makeup and nylons.

119

More than ever, the adolescent wants to be accepted—and not just by his parents but by his peers. He feels wretched at the sight of a pimple (even though every other kid in class has them, too). She cringes when she trips over her too-big feet, and she rearranges her hair a dozen times to hide ears that are too big for her face.

Saying, "Oh, honey, don't worry about it," isn't enough. We need to be the cheerleader once again.

"Mark, you're so strong. Will you open this jar for me?"

"Bill, it sure is good to have another man around the house!"

"Sally, I love the way you fixed your hair."

"Mary, blue is really your color."

Now don't get me wrong. Boys care about their appearance, too. This was news to me, until I had a teenager of my own. Steven had four hairstyles in two years. First he tried the traditional part on the side (my favorite). Then he moved on to the part down the middle. From there he went to no part at all. And finally he landed on the "messy" look.

When "messy" walked in the room, I could have said, "Yikes! You look awful! Go back and comb that hair right this minute!" But instead I said, "What exactly do you want your hair to look like?"

"Like this," he said, showing me a picture.

So I ruffled his bangs and showed him the fine art of using hair spray to keep the mess in place. (Yes, we fixed his hair to look as if it hadn't been fixed at all. Go figure!) Steven loved his messy hair and loved me for helping him. He blessed me ("You're way cool"), and I told him he looked handsome. At least it wasn't green! I don't prefer the messy look. However, Steven knew that I loved him unconditionally—even if I didn't like his hair. Besides, I know that, in a few more years, he will all too soon be parting his hair on the side and wearing a business suit.

Now, before you think I've gone crazy, I have sent him back to his room on a few occasions for what we call "excessive messiness." You have to draw the line somewhere, but make sure you're giving that teen as much freedom of expression as possible. After all, hair grows.

The Power of Liking

The foundation for building positive self-esteem is the kind of love God has for His children. This love isn't based on performance but on our just being His, and the Greek word for that love is *agape*. But another word

120

for *love* is also used in the Bible. Titus 2:4 tells us to "love [our] children" (NASB). The word used for *love* here is *phileo*, which means an affectionate love, a love that cherishes its object. It's friendship love (which is where Philadelphia, "the city of brotherly love," gets its name). It's a love that "likes" our children.[4]

I can't tell you how excited I became when I read about those two "love" words. So many children know their parents probably love them, but they don't believe their parents like them. Often, when a child doesn't measure up to his parents' expectations, moms and dads are quick to point out that child's faults and to tell how he could perform better, look better, and be better. As a result, the child's self-esteem rests on shaky ground, and he is easily toppled over by peers and the world around him.

I can't stress enough the need for children to know that they are liked by their parents. As adults, our perception of God is strongly influenced by how we perceive our parents. If a child sees his parents as dictators who exist to give red *X*s when he is bad and check marks when he is good, then he will see God as a judge to be feared and not as a loving Father to be revered. As a result of programming from their parents, many adults feel that God loves them, all right. He has to. He's God. But they don't think God likes them.

During the many years when I dropped Steven off at school, I would say, "'Bye. I love you, and I like you!" It always brought a smile. I wanted Steven to know this: "I like you. I like the person you are. I like being with you and playing games with you. I think you are funny, witty, intelligent, and fun to be around. If I were your age, I'd want you to be my best friend. I like being your mom!"

When Steven was about ten, we were visiting a neighbor who had several children. She said in the children's hearing, "I hate summer! These kids are driving me crazy. I can't wait until they're back in school." Of course the kids laughed, but I bet they were crying on the inside.

As we walked away, I put an arm around my son and said, "Steven, I love summer. I dread when school starts and I won't get to see you all day." I'm fortunate to have a son I easily and sincerely like, and I know some mothers' personalities clash with one or more of their children's personalities. These moms have a much bigger challenge before them, but God can help them to find ways to accentuate the positive, which every child has.

When a child feels unconditionally loved and accepted, he has a sense of security that encourages him to express how he feels about various subjects. When he talks, what do you get to do, oh, blessed mother? Listen! If he doesn't feel unconditionally loved and accepted, he will keep his opinions to himself for fear of rejection or isolation.

A Safe Place

Such feelings come soon enough for our kids. The world isn't a friendly place. I still remember being the last chosen for the kickball team, the party invitation that didn't come, being called "Queen Victoria" because I wouldn't give away a kiss. Rejection is a part of life, but we can make home a place where broken hearts are mended and frowns are turned upside down. Let's make sure that the foundation of unconditional love is so sound that the strong winds of rejection won't blow the house down.

Here's a version of 1 Corinthians 13 that can help each of us remember that building that foundation is the heart of our construction job:

If I keep my house spotless and dust free, and deliver crisp starched shirts and clean white socks, but do not show love to my family, I'm just another housewife.

If I cook well-balanced meals, pack delicious lunches, and prepare gourmet holiday dinners with all the trimmings, but do not show love to my family, I'm just another cook.

If I sew gorgeous window treatments, with matching fringed pillows and coordinating wall coverings, but do not show love to those who live therein, I am just another interior decorator.

Love puts down the dustcloth to hug the child. Love rubs a back, kisses a bruised knee, bandages a skinned elbow. Love colors a picture, plays cowboys and Indians, listens to endless stories.

Love is patient and kind, though weary and tired. Love doesn't envy another's child who never seems to misbehave, or get puffed up on the one occasion when hers doesn't. Love doesn't yell or swat but disciplines with control.

Cook, clean, and love. But the greatest of these is love.

CHAPTER FOURTEEN

The Framework: Capable, Valuable, with a Sense of Belonging

I was having lunch with four friends when the conversation turned to personality types. My vivacious, blonde friend Brenda could be the poster child for the sanguine personality. She is outgoing, never meets a stranger, is bubbly, and generally positive. But I knew Brenda's background and that she had a very critical mother. Brenda didn't see herself as sanguine at all.

"Brenda, you're definitely a sanguine!" the group chorused.

"How can you say that?" she asked. "If I'm a sanguine, why am I so insecure?"

"Being a sanguine is how God made you. Being insecure is how your mother made you," I answered.

In my work with women through The Proverbs 31 Ministry, I come in contact with so many women with poor self-esteem who feel they don't have what it takes to be a good wife or mother. When I dig deeper to find out the source of their insecurities, I find that many grew up with a mother who always had "a better way." If Susie was cooking a meal, her mother would come in and show her how to cook it better. If Susie was making the bed, her mother would come in and show her how to properly fold the corners under the mattress so the sheets would "hang right." One woman came home and found her visiting mother rearranging her den furniture. Undoubtedly, this lady had disturbed more than the furniture in her now-grown daughter's self-confidence.

Capable to Succeed

To build self-esteem in our children, we must make them feel capable. Are your little girl's bows crooked because she put them on? Praise her for her independence. Did your son miss a few spots when he washed the car? Thank him for helping around the house. If we want to make our kids feel capable, we must praise their efforts and not just point out how they could have done it "more perfectly." Which is more important, bringing to a boy's attention the few sprigs of grass he missed when he mowed the lawn or building confidence and a sense of accomplishment?

In building self-esteem, we must let perfection go. Of course the bed looks better when you make it, and the bathroom mirror has less white specks when you clean it. But what is your ultimate goal—teaching responsibility and creating a sense of accomplishment, or a spotless house?

Some moms might say, "Well, if I don't point out the faults, how will they ever learn to do it right?"

I guess it depends on what you're trying to build, perfect kids or children who feel capable. I believe that when a mother praises a child for a job well done, it makes him or her want to do it even better next time.

I'll admit, it's easier to do everything for your kids. It's quicker and a lot less painful. But the end result is a child who doesn't feel capable of performing even the simplest tasks.

The Little Engine That Could is a dynamo with self-esteem. But suppose, when the little engine started to climb that hill, struggling to tug the train over the mountain, his mommy engine came chugging along. Seeing poor little Junior huffing and puffing, she came to the rescue and pushed Junior over the hill. Well, he wouldn't have tooted off singing, "I thought I could! I thought I could! I thought I could!"

When a child feels capable, even failure is seen in proper perspective—like the time a neighbor heard a little boy talking to himself as he strode through his backyard, baseball cap in place and toting ball and bat.

"I'm the greatest baseball player in the world," he said proudly. Then he tossed the ball in the air, swung, and missed.

Undaunted, he picked up the ball, threw it in the air, and said to himself, "I'm the greatest player ever!"

He swung at the ball again, and again he missed. He paused a moment to examine the bat and ball carefully.

Then once again he threw the ball into the air and said, "I'm the greatest baseball player who ever lived."

He swung the bat hard and again missed the ball. "Wow!" he exclaimed. "What a pitcher!"[1]

Some mom had done a good job!

Author and mom Linda Webber notes, "What we build into our kids' hearts underpins what they live out in their lives. It has little to do with how much we give them. It has everything to do with how we make them feel."[2]

That's the same sentiment this poem expresses.

What Children Need

Children need more than clothes on their backs,
A roof o'er their heads and lunch in their sacks.
Children need more than cable TV,
The latest Nintendo, and videos to see.
Children need more than a beautiful home,
A roomful of toys and their own telephone.
Children need more than far-off vacations,
Amusement park rides and grand celebrations.
Though treasures we buy bring them smiles—it is true;
Our children need less than we might think they do.
Children need time to talk and to share,
For growing is painful and not always fair.
Children need someone with listening ears
To hear how their day went and help calm their fears.
Children need space, a home where there's rest,

A place where they're needed and told, "You're the best!"
Children need hands to hold when they're scared;
Children need arms to hug them and care.
Yes, children need less than we might think they do;
Children need love—Your children need you.

—Nancy Aguilar[3]

Children need moms to make them feel unconditionally loved, accepted, capable, valued, and of great worth. When a child feels incompetent in one area, other areas of his life are affected.

One day I was helping in Steven's second-grade classroom. The teacher held up a picture of a man raking leaves and two children playing in the background. The students were instructed to write a story about the picture. I walked around the room, noticing that most of the kids were writing pretty much the same scenario.

"It was Saturday. Mom was inside cooking breakfast. Dad was raking leaves. The children were playing."

I looked over at my son, and tears were streaming down his cheeks. As a rule, I didn't help Steven in his class, so his teacher went to see what the problem was.

"I have a story, but I don't know how to write it down," he declared in frustration.

"So tell me the story," his teacher said.

Steven began to weave his tale. "I am a leaf. There's a man coming after me. He wants to put me in a bag. 'Help! Help!' said the leaf. 'I don't want to go into the bag!'"

Steven went on for several minutes with a first-person story of how one little leaf felt about being tossed in a pile and eventually in the bag. His creative ability was years beyond what his physical and mental ability could record on paper.

It would have been so easy for the teacher to say, "Just write a nice little story like all the other kids. Don't cause trouble here." But instead, the teacher and I made a way for him to get his words down on paper and encouraged his individuality and creativity.

A sad twist to this story is that, even though Steven was very capable in many areas, he was a poor speller. The problem was so bad that his teacher suggested we have him tested for learning disabilities. The test concluded he had a visual perception problem, which meant he wasn't learning by simply seeing a word repeatedly.

The next year the school suggested he take a special program for his disability. Twice a week he was taken out of class to attend a forty-five-minute session. The teacher explained to Steven that he was very bright, but he had this one little problem.

Steven didn't buy that at all. He felt stupid. He was embarrassed to be taken out of class. Because he felt incapable, it affected every area of his life, and insecurity set in like a thick fog.

I prayed for wisdom and understanding and sought knowledge. I could see Steven's self-esteem rapidly declining. Three months later, I took him somewhere else to be tested.

"Mrs. Jaynes," the tester said, "Steven does not have a learning disability. He is a poor speller. He uses small words when he writes because he is afraid of misspelling the larger ones. Buy him a spell checker and take him out of that class before they cause irreparable damage to his self-esteem."

It took until the next school year for him to regain steady footing. But his confidence returned. He was inducted into the National Honor Society in junior high and took honors classes in high school. But I'd gotten my first taste of what can happen to a child when he feels that he isn't a capable person.

Actually, it wasn't my first taste. I remember from my own life how feelings of ineptness in first grade colored my view of myself. Just thinking about the first-grade "spelling train" makes me break into a cold sweat. In this torturous exercise, the students placed their little wooden chairs in a line to form a train. My teacher held up a card with a spelling word on it. If the person at the front of the train missed the word, she had to go to the back of the line. I spent most of my days in the caboose. One word that was a stumbling block for me was the word *the*. I missed it so many times, the teacher made me wear a piece of tape stuck to the front of my dress for two weeks with "the" written on it. Kids would come up, point, and say, "Is your name 'The'?"

Needless to say, I learned how to spell "the." But unfortunately, that's not all I learned. I figured out I was a poor speller. Ask my editor. She'll tell you.

But eventually, I learned that my worth wasn't based on whether I can perform every task well. (And praise the Lord for spell check.)

Unfortunately, weakness in an area can paralyze many kids (and adults). It's a mom's job to point her children to their strengths.

Steven is still a poor speller, but he is an incredible writer who continues to amaze his mom. Look for those special gifts and talents in your child and give him permission to take flight, using those gifts.

William Barclay tells this story of a mom who did just that. One day Benjamin West's mother went to run some errands, leaving him in charge of his little sister, Sally. In his mother's absence, he discovered some bottles of colored ink, and, to amuse Sally, he began to paint her portrait. As he worked, he made quite a mess, spilling ink splotches here and there.

When his mother returned, she saw the mess but said nothing. Instead, she picked up the piece of paper. Smiling, she exclaimed, "Why, it's Sally!" She then stooped and kissed her son. From that time on, Benjamin West would say, "My mother's kiss made me a painter."[4]

Many times a child doesn't act capable because he is treated as though he isn't. Goethe said, "Treat a man as he appears to be, and you make him worse. But treat a man as if he already were what he potentially could be, and you make him what he should be."[5]

A study was done in a classroom by Robert Rosenthal, a Harvard psychologist, and Lenore Jacobson, a San Francisco school principal, that illustrates Goethe's point. A group of kindergarten through fifth-grade students was given a learning ability test. The next fall the new teachers were casually told the names of five or six children who were designated as "spurters." The tests supposedly revealed that they had exceptional learning ability.

Unbeknownst to the teachers, the names of the spurters had been chosen randomly. At the end of the school year, all the students were retested. The pupils whom the teachers thought had the most potential had gained fifteen to twenty-seven IQ points. Plus, the teachers described these children as happier, more curious, more affectionate, and having a better chance of success in later life than the average student. But the only change in that school year from the one before was the teachers' attitude. Because the teachers expected more of certain students, those children came to expect more of themselves.

"The explanation probably lies in the subtle interaction between teacher and pupils," speculated psychologist Rosenthal. "Tone of voice, facial expressions, touch, and posture may be the means by which—often unwittingly—teachers communicate their expectations to their pupils. Such communication may help a child by changing his perceptions of himself."[6]

Capable to Decide

One way to build confidence and self-esteem is to allow a child to make decisions. Of course, this privilege increases with age and maturity. In the first eight years of a child's life, parents basically are in control, giving the child a choice between two good options. "Would you like to wear your red coat or your blue sweater today?" When the child is between ages eight and sixteen, she is allowed to make more choices, with the parent as a coach who guides.

Once the child is sixteen to twenty-two years old, the parents act as counselors, snipping those apron strings and granting independence. During this period, some bad choices probably will be made. No mom wants her child to fail. However, part of feeling capable is learning to make responsible decisions. And part of making responsible decisions is occasionally to make poor ones. Wouldn't you prefer that those bad decisions be made while the child is still at home rather than when she is away from the love and support of those who value her for who she is?

Capable to Achieve

When Steven was fifteen, we were window-shopping and strolled up to a music store. He was drawn into its doors by a shiny silver electric guitar with three toning knobs, a double hum bucker, and classic curves. The store owner lowered the hallowed stringed instrument from its mount on the wall and placed it in Steven's admiring hands. She plugged in the amplifier, and the room came alive with rhythm as Steven's nimble fingers glided over the frets and wires. Then Steven's heart sank as he flipped over the price tag: $300.

"Oh, well," he said, handing the guitar back to the shop owner. "Thanks for letting me play."

As we walked out of the music store, I said, "You know, if you cut three lawns a week for five weeks, that silver-stringed lady could be yours."

The wheels in his head started to turn, and, shortly thereafter, the wheels on the lawn mower started to roll. Six weeks later, he walked into the music store, took the guitar off the wall, and proudly handed over his wad of ten-dollar bills to the proprietor.

Steven gained more than a guitar that day. He left with a feeling of accomplishment and personal worth. He had set a goal and had found he could achieve it. Now, when he strums those strings, he is stroking his self-esteem as well.

Valuable

Once Martha Taft was asked to introduce herself to her elementary school classmates. She stood and said, "My name is Martha Bowers Taft. My great-grandfather was president of the United States. My grandfather was a United States senator. My daddy is ambassador to Ireland. And I am a Brownie."[7] Undoubtedly, someone had taught Martha she had great value.

Making our children feel a sense of worth is paramount in building self-esteem. If we're watchful Beacons and Listeners and Encouragers, we will make our children feel valued.

However, nothing is more powerful in battling feelings of insecurity, inadequacy, and inferiority than a solid understanding of who we are, what we have, and where we are in Christ. We can try the best we can to build self-esteem, but Scripture says, "Unless the Lord builds the house, its builders labor in vain" (Psalm 127:1). We can help, but ultimately a person's true value is found in Jesus Christ.

Moms, these thoughts are for you too. Deuteronomy says, "[Moms,] you shall love the Lord your God with all your heart and with all your soul and with all your might. And these words, which I am commanding you today, shall be on *your* heart; and you shall teach them diligently to your sons . . ." (6:5–7 NASB). Before we can instill in our children a biblical understanding of how valuable they are, we must grasp how valuable *we* are to God.

All too often we hear that we are sinners saved by grace. And what a wonderful truth that is. But what comes after we've come to that realization? What does God have to say about who we are once we've found our way to Him?

These questions remind me of a story I heard once about a little boy who scampered off to bed one night. Not too long after he had turned out the lights, his mother heard a loud thud. She ran into his room to check on him. "What happened?" she asked.

"I don't know. I guess I stayed too close to where I got in," the boy answered as he scrambled back into bed.

Let's not stay too close to where we got in, but let's continue to grow in the knowledge of who we are in Christ. Look over the following list and embrace what God says about your identity in Christ.

Who Am I?

- I am the salt of the earth (Matthew 5:13).
- I am the light of the world (Matthew 5:14).
- I am a child of God (John 1:12).
- I am part of the true Vine, a channel (branch) of Christ's life (John 15:5).
- I am Christ's friend (John 15:15).
- I am chosen and appointed by Christ to bear His fruit (John 15:16).
- I am a slave of righteousness (Romans 6:18).
- I am a joint-heir with Christ, sharing His inheritance with Him (Romans 8:14–17).
- I am God's temple. His Spirit dwells in me (1 Corinthians 3:16).
- I am joined to the Lord and am one spirit with Him (1 Corinthians 6:17).
- I am a member (part) of Christ's body (1 Corinthians 12:27).
- I am a new creation (2 Corinthians 5:17).
- I am reconciled to God and am a minister of reconciliation (2 Corinthians 5:18–19).
- I am a son of God and one with other believers (Galatians 3:26, 28).
- I am an heir of God, since I am a son of God (Galatians 4:6–7).
- I am a saint (Ephesians 1:1).
- I am God's workmanship, created in Christ to do His work that He planned all along for me to do (Ephesians 2:10).
- I am a fellow citizen with the rest of God's family (Ephesians 2:19).
- I am righteous and holy (Ephesians 4:24).
- I am a citizen of heaven (Philippians 3:20).
- I am an expression of Christ because He is in me (Colossians 3:4).
- I am chosen by God, holy, and dearly loved (Colossians 3:12).
- I am a child of light and not of darkness (1 Thessalonians 5:5).

- I am one of God's living stones and am being built into a spiritual house with the rest of the believers (1 Peter 2:5).
- I am part of a chosen people, a royal priesthood, a holy nation, a people belonging to God, whose purpose is to praise Him (1 Peter 2:9–10).
- I am an alien and stranger to this world in which I temporarily live (1 Peter 2:11).
- I am an enemy of the devil (1 Peter 5:8).
- I will resemble Christ when He returns (1 John 3:2).
- I am born of God, and the "evil one," the devil, cannot harm me (1 John 5:18).
- I am not the great I AM, but by the grace of God I am what I am (1 Corinthians 15:10).

Mom, you are somebody! And nothing you can do for your children to build their confidence is more important than ushering them into God's kingdom and introducing them to the One who loves them most. That's the best way to ensure feelings of worth.

If your child already has made a commitment to Christ, read and reread this list to him or her. Deuteronomy 6 says to bind the Word on your forehead and on your child's and to write it on your doorpost. But I think taping it on the family's bathroom mirror will work splendidly!

I hope one day I'll hear my son introduce himself this way: "Hello, my name is Steven Jaynes. My great-grandfather was a farmer. One grandfather was a builder, and the other was a high school football coach. My father was a dentist. And I am a child of God, the salt of the earth, who has been blessed with every spiritual blessing in the heavenlies."

A Place to Belong

Do you remember the children's story *Are You My Mother?* A little chick is born, but he can't find his mother. Throughout the book, he scampers up to different animals and asks, "Are you my mother?" The little bird knew he belonged somewhere, but he just wasn't sure where.[8]

Each child is born with a need to belong. We want to belong to a team, a clique, a person, and, most important, a family. God has created us with the desire to become part of a unit. Genealogies were important in the Bible; they showed that individuals were connected to something greater than themselves.

For our children to have high self-esteem, they need to have a sense of belonging. A child wants to feel he is needed and is a vital part of the family. Kids need to hear messages such as "I need you to clean your room." "I need you to feed the dog." "I need you to help make major decisions in our family." Even though a child might complain when we ask her to take part in the running of a household, it causes her to develop a sense of belonging. Children learn that without their help the household wouldn't run as smoothly; they are a contributing part of a team.

One day a lawn-care service provider stopped by and looked over our one-acre yard. "You need a lawn-care service for this yard," he said.

"What for?" my husband replied. "We have a son."

At that moment I'll bet our son felt capable, valuable, and that he belonged. And maybe—just for a millisecond—he wished he didn't.

CHAPTER FIFTEEN

$\mathcal{A}$dding Insulation,
Locks, and Bolts

*W*hen I was in college, I lived in an old drafty apartment. During the winter, the curtains moved when the wind blew outside, even though the windows were closed. No matter how high we turned the thermostat, the rooms were never warm enough. It had nothing to do with the heating system but everything to do with the insulation.

A blessed mother is one who wraps her loving arms around her child to insulate him against the chilly winds of the world. She rubs in security as she rubs a back and pats in value as she pats a shoulder. She smooths jostled emotions as she ruffles hair. Love is the foundation we can give our children, a sense of competence is the framework, and affection is the insulation.

Can a person receive too many hugs and kisses? I don't think so. A blessed mother greets her children with a kiss in the morning and seals the day with a hug at night. And those tough boys need it just as much as those sweet girls. Studies show that six-year-old boys receive one-sixth as much hugging and kissing as six-year-old girls, and six-year-old boys get into six times more trouble than six-year-old girls.[1]

Psychologists have shown that hugs can add years to a life and a lack of affection can lead to a lack of health. Dr. Ross Campbell studied this phenomenon, called Failure to Thrive Syndrome, in a university hospital. Children with this illness, usually between six and twelve months old, stop developing, become listless, and often stop eating. Many of the children Dr. Campbell observed died, even though physically they appeared normal. In most cases, the child's parents, many times unconsciously, rejected the child and avoided eye contact and physical contact. They provided food and clothing but no affection.[2] Affection is vital to a child's development, both emotionally and physically.

Cuddling an infant is easy, but what about that fifth grader or that standoffish teen? Do they need affection? Yes, indeed.

Another study showed that 54 percent of mothers gave daily verbal affirmation such as "I love you" to their fifth graders, but by the time the child was in ninth grade, only 36 percent of the mothers were doing so. As for physical affection such as hugs, kisses, and pats on the back, 68 percent of the mothers displayed affection to their fifth graders, but by the time the child was in ninth grade, the hugs and kisses had dropped to 44 percent.[3]

Unfortunately, during the time adolescents are struggling with personal identity and self-esteem, parents are withholding verbal and physical affection. I can almost feel the chill creeping through the windowsills and under the door's threshold.

Don't let those adolescents fool you. They may pull away when you reach to give them a hug, but it's usually because they're feeling the tug to be independent and a desire to be "cool." Hug them anyway. Deep down, they don't want you to stop.

Don't let the rebuffs hurt your feelings. They are normal. Of course, you do have to pick your time and place. Public displays of affection can be embarrassing to a teen, and you need to "honor his dignity." But don't think for a moment that the beautiful young lady or the six-foot, muscle-bound young man doesn't need your comforting arms to reassure him or her of your love, acceptance, and esteem—that your teen is the apple of your eye.

Locks on the Windows and Bolts on the Doors

When I was in my early twenties, I lived for one year in the upstairs apartment of my parents' home. They were gone much of the time, and the living arrangement gave me a chance to cushion my bank account for my impending independence.

One night my father was out of town, and my mother was at a meeting. I was dressing to go out for the evening and putting on the final touches of makeup in the bathroom. I heard a rattling outside the window, so I turned out the light to get a better view. What did I see but a man on a ladder peering in the window at me!

Somehow I managed to run down the stairs, out the front door, by the man's parked car, and over to a neighbor's house. I'm convinced the Lord sent angels to propel my paralyzed body forward. I burst into our neighbor's house and just stood there, ashen and unable to speak. Finally, I managed to tell her that a man was at my bathroom window. The police came, but of course the perpetrator was long gone. All that remained was the ladder leaning against the house.

It was one of the most frightening experiences of my life, especially when I realized that this window was the only one in the entire house that didn't have a lock. The upstairs apartment was a later addition, and somehow we just never got around to putting a lock on that last sash.

First Peter 5:8 says, "Be self-controlled and alert. Your enemy the devil prowls around like a roaring lion looking for someone to devour." He seeks to "steal and kill and destroy" (John 10:10) our children, and, just as he attacked Jesus in the desert after forty days of fasting, so he will attack our children at their weakest points.

Satan's game plan always has been to look for the unsecured window. He tauntingly says, "Go ahead and lie. If you tell the truth, you'll get in big trouble." "A few cigarettes won't hurt anything." "Go ahead and drink a few beers. Your friends will think you're cool." "One snort won't hurt anything. It'll be fun." "Go ahead and swear. It'll show you're tough." "Go ahead and sleep with that guy. He loves you. He said so." "Besides, everybody's doing it . . . doing it . . . doing it . . ."

We know the lies because we've heard them before. Many of us remember the lies, and we bear the scars from when we believed them ourselves.

Satan's greatest weapon among children today is peer pressure. Dr. James Dobson explains it this way:

There are two great forces that combine to create havoc during adolescence, the first having hormonal origin. The other is social in nature. It is common knowledge that a twelve- or thirteen-year-old child suddenly awakens to a brand new world around him, as though his eyes were opening for the first time. The world is populated by age mates who scare him out of his wits. His greatest anxiety, far exceeding the fear of death, is the possibility of rejection or humiliation in the eyes of his peers. . . . It is impossible to comprehend the adolescent mind without understanding the terror of the peer group.[4]

The Bible says, "As iron sharpens iron, so one man sharpens another" (Proverbs 27:17). When I was in high school, I had a group of Christian friends who held me accountable, helped me to resist temptation, and inspired me to develop a deeper walk with God. As mothers, we can pray that our children will each have at least one friend to stand with them in their convictions. Better yet, make it two.

Shadrach, Meshach, and Abednego understood the power of having a friend to stand with them. When most of their countrymen were murdered by King Nebuchadnezzar in 605 B.C., these three were taken captive to live in the king's household. They were educated and offered the cuisine of the king's court. However, they decided to stick to their convictions and refuse to eat those tasty steaks that were roasting on the fire and that full-bodied wine as the carafe was passed under their noses. They were tempted to give up their vegetarian ways, but their accountability group of three kept each of them strong. When they had to choose whether to bow down to the king's idol or continue to honor God, they decided to follow God, even if it meant death. You know the rest of the story: The boys were thrown into the fiery furnace, but God miraculously saved them.

Today, children typically aren't thrown into a fiery furnace. They are thrown into school. We need to pray for friends that will go the distance—even to the fiery furnace.

We can't lock our kids in the house to protect them from the Enemy's assaults. But we can give them the tools to recognize and fight his tactics. We can build self-esteem with a solid foundation of unconditional love and acceptance, a strong framework that makes them feel capable, valuable, and with a sense of belonging. We can insulate them with plenty of warm affection and teach them how to put locks on the windows and bolts on the doors. Then, when the big bad wolf comes snooping around, he can huff and puff, but he won't be able to blow the house down.

A Roof of Prayer

Building self-esteem in children is no easy task. We definitely can't hand the job over to a subcontractor such as a coach, youth group leader, or a teacher. The wise woman builds her house. She uses wisdom, understanding, and knowledge. And she covers it all in prayer, just as a roof tops a house. The most elaborately built dwelling would soon be in shambles without a solid roof to keep out the elements. So it is with prayer. A blessed mother points her children to the Master Builder Himself.

In *You Are Special,* Max Lucado tells the story of a village consisting of wooden people called "Wemmicks." They go around sticking stars on people who are beautiful and who can perform great tasks, such as picking up big sticks. And they stick dots on people who have chipped paint or make mistakes. Punchinello is a wooden person who has lots of dots, but he meets someone who has no dots and no stars. When he asks her about why the stickers don't stick to her, she says it's because she meets with the woodcarver, Eli, each day. Finally Punchinello works up enough courage to go see Eli, his creator.

Right off, Punchinello apologizes for all his dots, but Eli says, "Oh, you don't have to defend yourself to me, child. I don't care what the other Wemmicks think. And you shouldn't either. Who are they to give stars or dots? They're Wemmicks just like you. What they think doesn't matter. All that matters is what I think. And I think you're pretty special."

Punchinello laughs. "Me? Special? Why? I can't walk fast. I can't jump. My paint is peeling. Why do I matter to you?"

Eli looks at Punchinello, puts his hands on those small wooden shoulders, and speaks very slowly. "Because, you're mine. That's why you matter to me. . . . And remember, I don't make mistakes."

Punchinello doesn't understand at first, but as he leaves, in his heart he thinks, *I think he really means it.* With that thought, a dot falls to the ground.[5]

So add the covering of prayer to shelter your child, and pray that he will discover how much his Creator values him. Pray that he will realize that what God thinks about him is more important than what anyone else thinks—and that God thinks he is special. That's the true key to building self-esteem.

REHEARSING THE SCENE

As blessed moms, we can strengthen our children's arsenal with Scripture and give them the tools to say no. Role-play situations with your children ahead of time. Then, when the curtain goes up and the spotlight is in their faces, they will be able to say no with confidence.

Practice these scenarios:

- If you were in the car with your boyfriend, and his hand started to go places it shouldn't, what would you do?
- If you went to a party and people were drinking, what would you do?
- If you were walking through the mall and your friend slipped some gum into his pocket without paying for it, what would you do?
- If you were with friends and one of them pulled out a pack of cigarettes, what would you say?
- If your best friend wanted to look at your answers on a test, what would you do?
- What would you do if a group of guys called you a sissy, a baby, a momma's boy, or a coward for not following the crowd?

Use these ideas to help build strong self-esteem in your child:

- Celebrate special achievements by letting your child eat on "the special plate." At our house we have a red plate that reads "You Are Special Today" around the perimeter. On special days, such as birthdays, the person of honor eats off the red plate. I even take a picture and keep a "Red Plate Photo Album."
- Provide opportunities for your child to achieve success such as a school play or earning Scout badges.
- Include your child in planning family activities.
- If your child has a knack for design, allow him to rearrange the furniture in his room or to paint the room.
- Help your child to set realistic goals and to reach them.
- Thank your child for helping around the house.
- Make a scrapbook to chronicle important events.
- Make a big picture book using 8 x 10 photos from school and sports teams.
- Record and watch home videos of your child.
- Create a birthday memory book with a photo of each year and recordings of major events.
- Frame your young child's artwork and display it in your home.
- Help your child to open a savings account with her own money.

- Encourage your child to do jobs around the neighborhood, such as cut grass, water plants, walk pets, baby-sit, and pick up mail for those on vacation.
- Purchase or make a banner or flag for each child and fly it on his or her special days.
- Teach etiquette rules such as proper introductions, how to address an adult, when to extend a hand for a handshake, which eating utensil to use for which course, when to stand when a lady approaches. Good manners give a child and young adult confidence in social settings. If you aren't sure of the rules yourself, read an etiquette book and learn them together.
- Create a "sick tray" to use when you serve a child who is under the weather. Include a special plate, a flower, and a candle.
- End your phone conversations when your child walks in from school.
- Assign your child a household project: painting the garage, raking the leaves, sweeping the sidewalks.
- Build a model airplane together.
- Teach your child how to play a sport well.
- Touch your child when you talk.
- Give lots of hugs. Give lots of kisses. Put a chocolate kiss in your child's lunch box.
- Catch your child doing something right at least twice a day.
- Read *The Emperor's New Clothes* and ask why no one was willing to tell the king he was naked.

- Have young children put away their toys when they are fin-ished playing with them.
- Make older children responsible for keeping their rooms tidy.
- Provide a tutor if your child has an academic struggle.
- Let your child pick out her own clothes.
- Don't finish your child's sentences for him.
- Don't allow your child to use self-criticism such as "I'm so ugly," "I'm stupid," or "I can't do it."
- Allow mistakes.
- Cut apron strings gradually, but cut you must.
- Help your child start an at-home business such as a lemonade stand or window washing.
- Teach your son or daughter a new skill, such as baking a cake or changing a tire.
- Allow your child to contribute financially to a family purchase.
- Listen to your child practice a musical instrument.
- Ask your child's opinion on a big family decision.
- Help your daughter fix her hair.
- Decorate your child's locker door on his birthday.
- Send a balloon-o-gram to school on your child's birthday.
- Take lots of pictures.

CHAPTER SIXTEEN

Nancy Hanks Lincoln: A Self-Esteem-Building Mother

If ever a man should have felt bad about himself, it was Abraham Lincoln. After all, he failed in business in '31, he was defeated for the legislature and lost his job in '32, he was elected to the legislature in '34 but had a nervous breakdown in '36, was defeated for speaker in '38, was defeated for elector in '40, was defeated for Congress in '43, was elected to Congress in '46 but defeated in '48, was defeated by less than one hundred votes for the Senate in '50, was defeated for vice president in '56 and for the Senate in '58. But in 1860 he was elected president of the United States. After losing a Senate race, Lincoln said, "The path was worn and slippery. My foot slipped from under me, knocking the other out of the way, but I recovered and said to myself, 'It's a slip and not a fall.'"[1]

Someone once asked Abe about his tenacity to persevere in the face of so many defeats. He stated that he considered his mother to be chiefly responsible for all he was and ever hoped to become.[2] He rose up and called her blessed.

Who was this powerhouse of a mother? Just a poor, simple, country woman who had little to offer in material goods but much to give in spiritual and emotional wisdom. She taught her son to read *the Bible* and to continue on in the face of failure. Amazingly, she did all this before Abe's eleventh birthday, for she died when he was ten.

Mothers of young children, never underestimate your influence in the early years. Abe said, "I remember my mother's prayers, and they have always followed me. They have clung to me all of my life."[3] He also said, "No one is poor who has a godly mother."[4]

We have Mary Hanks Lincoln to thank for providing our nation with a godly president who had such a strong sense of self-esteem that he was able to lead our nation through its most terrible years, the years in which it lost its way and became a house divided against itself.

TWO TEMPLES

A builder built a temple,
He wrought it with grace and skill;
Pillars and groins and arches
All fashioned to work his will.
Men said as they saw its beauty,
"It shall never know decay;
Great is thy skill, O Builder!
Thy fame shall endure for aye."

A mother built a temple
With loving and infinite care,
Planning each arch with patience,
Laying each stone with prayer.
None praised her unceasing efforts,
None knew of her wondrous plan,
For the temple the mother built
Was unseen by the eyes of man.

Gone is the builder's temple,
Crumbled into the dust;
Low lies each stately pillar,
Food for consuming rust.
But the temple the mother built
Will last while the ages roll,
For that beautiful unseen temple
Was a child's immortal soul.

—Hattie Vose Hall
Used by permission of
Berg Christian Enterprises

If Virtue alone is happiness . . . never was an existence upon earth more blessed than my mother's.

—John Quincy Adams

When Napoleon was asked to identify the one thing that would restore the prestige and greatness of France, he offered only one solution: "Give us better mothers."

SECTION FIVE

Be a
Seed Sower

CHAPTER SEVENTEEN

Tending
the Fields

*M*y grandfather was a farmer, and several of his children followed in his muddy footsteps. One thing I learned as a little girl while I watched my aunts and uncles is that the farmer never just plants the seeds, leaves them alone, and hopes for the best. No, he tends the land. With all the modern farm equipment today, such as combines, harrows, and harvesters, the word "tend" has lost some of its significance. But this precious word exemplifies a mother's "tend-er" care.

The mother whose children rise up and call her blessed is a Seed Sower. She gathers good seeds from God's Word and presses them into the fertile soil of her children's heart. She fertilizes the seeds with encouraging words, spurring them to grow to their fullest potential. And she waters the seeds daily with prayer. Then one day the tender shoots burst forth, resulting in a bounty of fruit, and the seed sower celebrates the rewards of her labor.

A hundred years ago, farmers cut furrows in the ground by walking behind the plow as Mildred the mule pulled it along. The farmer knelt on bended knee and pushed the seeds into the tilled soil with his bare hands. He didn't spray pre-emergents but hand-pulled weeds that threatened to choke out the young plants' life. If the weather turned cool and a late frost was a possibility, the farmer protected the shoots with a covering for the night. To keep predators at bay, he erected a scarecrow. The only irrigation system available was a direct pipeline from heaven, as the farmer and his family prayed for God to send life-giving rain to water the fields. That's nurturing. That's tending.

Webster defines *tend* as "to take care of, to look after, to stand by, to prevent fouling, and to give attention to." The blessed mother is a Seed Sower; a Beacon; an intent Listener to her child's needs, hopes, desires, and disappointments; and a Self-Esteem Builder who erects a foundation of love, making the child feel capable, valuable, and with a sense of belonging.

The idea of tending was threaded in a request Jesus made of Peter. After Peter had denied Jesus three times, Jesus asked, "Peter, do you love Me?" Following each of Peter's responses, "Lord, You know I love You," Jesus gave a directive. Twice He told Peter to feed His sheep, and once He said, "Take care of My sheep." I believe Jesus was distinguishing between meeting someone's physical needs and tending to his emotional and spiritual needs. And that's what a blessed mother does—she tends to all three areas, diligently "feeding" and "caring" for her lambs.

In Deuteronomy 6:7, Moses instructs parents to "impress" the Word on their children (NIV). *Impress* means "to point, to pierce, to prick, to teach diligently, or to whet." I like to think of it as pressing tiny seeds into the willing earth.

I just love the feel of freshly turned dirt in my hands. Each spring my husband admonishes me, "Put on those work gloves. You're going to ruin your hands." But using my bare fingers to press those tiny flower seeds under the ground and then pat the dirt back in place fills me with pleasure. I hope the neighbors can't hear me whispering a prayer over the little mounds.

A farmer would never simply scatter seeds and hope for the best. His tender care and labor ensures their growth. Likewise, a mother can't leave the spiritual growth of her children to chance. She must sow good seeds and nourish those seeds until her children leave home and venture off into responsible lives of their own.

But tending takes time. There's that old nemesis again—time.

Linda Webber in her book *Mom, You're Incredible* tells of an incident in which she and her husband were eating in a nice restaurant. Two women in their sixties sat down at a table near them. Though their dress and manners conveyed that these women "had it all together," one of them obviously was distressed. Because they were talking rather loudly, the Webbers overheard one woman pouring out her heart to her friend.

"My mother didn't care for me much as a little girl. She certainly wasn't home much, and when she was, she had very little time for me. I was pretty much left on my own. As a matter of fact, I had to take on most of the responsibilities that I saw my friends' mothers doing."[1]

This sixty-something woman still resented her mother's work because it seemed to be more important than she was. In this woman's mind, her mother never taught her anything, not even how to cook, much less how to live. And here she was, an older lady, still trying to resolve those feelings of not being cared for.

The time we spend today sowing seeds in our children's lives will reap a bountiful crop tomorrow. One day I was speaking on the telephone to the mother of an eight-month-old and a three-and-a-half-year-old. All during the conversation, both children were screaming. The baby was crying because she was a baby and that's what babies do, especially when Mommy is on the phone. The three-year-old was screaming because the baby was crying. All the while, I was trying to counsel this young mother about an in-law problem.

I talked, the kids screamed, and she tried to listen. Finally, I asked, "Honey, would you like for me to call you back at a better time?"

"There is no better time," she said, exasperated. "It's always like this."

I doubt it was "always" like that, but my heart went out to her. For a young mom, those times of frustration and exhaustion run together into one hazy blur of days. Erma Bombeck compared housework to stringing beads with no knot at the end. Some days, mothering feels the same way. I so wanted to give this young mother a hug and to comfort her with one of my favorite Bible verses, "And it came to pass" (Luke 2:1 KJV).

It does pass—quickly—and then the time for tending the field is over. No more toys to pick up. No more fingerprints to scrub from the walls. No more wet towels slung over the chair. Just silence.

Sow good seeds while you can. Tend the fields with care. Now is the time.

Time Is of the Essence

Now is the time to get things done . . .
wade in the water,
sit in the sun,
squish my toes
in the mud by the door,
explore the world with a boy just four.

Now is the time to study books,
flowers,
snails,
how a cloud looks;
to ponder "up,"
where God sleeps nights,
why mosquitoes take such big bites.
To sew and clean,
paint the hall
that soft new green
to make new drapes,
refinish the floor—
Later on . . . when he's not just four.

—Irene Foster[2]

Cultivating the Soil

In the sixth grade, I conducted a science experiment regarding the best environment for growing beans. (Sounds exciting, huh?) I planted lima beans in nine pots: three in rich topsoil, three in sand, three in clay. Then I placed one of each kind of soil in three different types of light: in full sunlight, a closet with light from a lone lightbulb, and one in a closet with no light at all.

Over the next few weeks, I plotted the beans' progress on a growth chart. Predictably, the beans in the dark closet didn't sprout at all, and the beans in both kinds of light fared well. But my prize bean came from the seed planted in the fertile topsoil that was nourished by sunlight.

Is the soil in your home like hard clay that stifles the roots from spreading? Does the soil hold too tightly, not allowing the water to flow, thus causing the seeds to rot?

Is the soil in your home sandy, with too much freedom, preventing the roots from grabbing hold? Is the environment too loosely structured, with boundaries that change like shifting sand?

Or is the soil in your home rich, with plenty of nutrients? Is it firm enough to allow the roots to take hold but loose enough to allow the roots to sink deep and spread wide?

Jesus talked about the importance of the soil in His parable of the sower:

A farmer went out to sow his seed. As he was scattering the seed, some fell along the path, and the birds came and ate it up. Some fell on rocky places, where it did not have much soil. It sprang up quickly, because the soil was shallow. But when the sun came up, the plants were scorched, and they withered because they had no root. Other seed fell among thorns, which grew up and choked the plants. Still other seed fell on good soil, where it produced a crop—a hundred, sixty or thirty times what was sown. (Matthew 13:3–8)

How can the blessed mother cultivate the soil so that it will accept the seeds? Jesus tells us when He explains the parable:

1. "When anyone hears the message about the kingdom and does not understand it, the evil one comes and snatches away what was sown in his heart. This is the seed sown along the path" (verse 19).

When you sow seeds in your child's heart, make sure that he understands the godly principle behind the instruction. Instead of simply saying, "Don't lie," explain that God is truth and that Satan is the father of lies with no truth in him. When we lie, we please Satan and dishonor God. Lying is wrong because God tells us not to. Help your child to understand not only principles to live by but also God's character, which underpins each principle.

2. "The one who received the seed that fell on rocky places is the man who hears the word and at once receives it with joy. But since he has no root, he lasts only a short time. When trouble or persecution comes because of the word, he quickly falls away" (verses 20–21).

Our children will go through rocky times of persecution and rejection because of their faith. They may even encounter rocky places where they doubt their belief in God. My son went through a time in the ninth grade when he had to decide if his faith was his parents' or his own. Was it scary for me to watch? Yes. But that was a pivotal time in his spiritual growth. During such moments, we can help pick through the rocks and pray for our children as they struggle down the road. Then, when the rocks are cleared, they can use them to build an altar to the Lord, reminding them of where they came from.

3. "The one who received the seed that fell among the thorns is the man who hears the word, but the worries of this life and the deceitfulness of wealth choke it, making it unfruitful" (verse 22).

As moms, we need to look for the thorns in our children's lives. I asked Steven where he thought most of the "weeds" in his life came from. Without hesitation he answered, "Friends and television," even though he watches very little TV.

Know your child's friends. Are they encouraging or hindering spiritual growth? Is a friend a thorn that needs to be plucked up and removed? This may be one of the hardest jobs as a parent. Removing thorns can be painful; sometimes the gardener loses blood.

I can remember when I was in the fifth grade and my mother forbade me to hang out with a certain group of girls. I was furious with her. The word "hate" probably came from my mouth. But that parenting decision was one of the best my mom ever made. Seven years later, one of those girls was involved in the occult, one had a baby in the school parking lot, and one died from kidney failure, the result of drug abuse. I didn't understand in fifth grade why my mom didn't like those girls. But she saw something that an eleven-year-old couldn't see. Somehow she knew the path those girls were headed toward was a dangerous one, and she plucked me from the thorns.

4. "But the one who received the seed that fell on good soil is the man who hears the word and understands it. He produces a crop, yielding a hundred, sixty or thirty times what was sown" (verse 23).

Finally, the good soil is an environment that helps the child understand the Word. The version of this parable that appears in Mark's gospel says he "accept[s] it" (4:20), while the Luke version says he "retain[s] it, and by persevering produce[s] a crop" (8:15).

In the end, we plant seeds and tend the soil, but the child must accept the Word. Then God causes the seeds to grow. Our job is to be the seed tender; the rest is between God and our child.

CHAPTER EIGHTEEN

Sowing Seeds
of Scripture
and Prayer

We all know that a seed-and-feed store displays in neatly arranged rows hundreds of seed packets for the industrious gardener. But imagine that, instead of lima beans, tomatoes, and cucumber seeds, the packets are labeled Character, Truth, Generosity, Hope, and Compassion. Which ones would you choose?

We can plant so many good seeds in our children's hearts, but in the next few pages, I want to focus on the ones found in the pages of God's Word. Paul wrote to his son in the Lord, Timothy, "All Scripture is inspired by God and profitable for teaching, for reproof, for correction, for training in righteousness; that the man of God may be adequate, equipped for every good work" (2 Timothy 3:16–17 NASB). The best textbook for life is God's Word, and no seeds are more powerful than Scripture.

In America's early years, schoolchildren learned their ABCs from *The New England Primer.* The alphabet was taught with a Bible verse for each letter. For example,

A wise son maketh a glad father, but a foolish son is the heaviness of his mother.

Better is a little with the fear of the Lord, than a great treasure and trouble therewith.

Come unto Christ all ye that labor and are heavy laden and He will give you rest.

Much has changed since *The New England Primer* of 1777, but, although our public schools don't incorporate God's Word into the curriculum, we can make sure we sow seeds of Scripture at home. Elizabeth George, author of *A Woman After God's Own Heart,* tells of one mother who recited the Scripture she was memorizing to her little ones each night as she tucked them into bed. Many years later, one of her college-age daughters exclaimed, "I don't even know how I learned so much Scripture by heart. I guess I've just heard my mother say it over my bed so often that I picked it up!"

Elizabeth George goes on to say:

This mother, who both valued being a mother and treasured God's Word, recited lengthy passages and even entire psalms and books of the Bible to her children at bedtime. When her son was playing basketball in college, he made it a practice to go into the gymnasium before each game, lie down on a bleacher, and recite Romans six through eight to calm his nerves and focus his heart on God. Their son's fiancée told me that, on her holiday visits to his home, this godly mother also tucked her into bed, reciting Scripture and praying with her—at age twenty-two—as she made the rounds to all of her adult children's rooms.[1]

Sowing seeds that teach about God can be as natural as breathing: praising God for a beautiful sunset, thanking Him for our food, praying for a skinned knee. We start the planting as soon as the child is born. When you rock the babe in your arms, tell her how much Jesus loves her. When you bathe him in the sink, tell about how Jesus washes away our sins. When you comb her hair, tell about how God knows every hair on her head.

We can use everyday parables. For example, at dinner one night, prepare mashed potatoes with no salt. Suggest that the kids taste them and then ask, "What's wrong with the potatoes? That's right. They have no flavor. Now let's add some salt. How do they taste? Jesus says that we are the salt of the earth. Why do you think He called us that?"

When I worked in a medical office several years ago, we had what we called "tray setups." On the trays were all the instruments we needed for various procedures. They were prepared ahead of time and stored in a cabinet. When a patient came in for a certain procedure, I didn't have to scramble around to find what I needed. I simply walked to the cabinet and pulled out the prepared tray.

In the same way, Scripture memorization is preparation for the future. When you and your child have Scripture hidden in your hearts, you can "pull out" the exact verse when you need it. Here are some tools you might need:

- When you are afraid
  "For God did not give us a spirit of timidity; but a spirit of power, of love and of self-discipline" (2 Timothy 1:7).
- When you are angry
  "A gentle answer turns away wrath, but a harsh word stirs up anger" (Proverbs 15:1).
- When you are confused
  "I will instruct you and teach you in the way you should go; I will counsel you and watch over you" (Psalm 32:8).
- When you are frustrated
  "Commit to the Lord whatever you do, and your plans will succeed" (Proverbs 16:3).
- When someone hurts you
  "Be kind and compassionate to one another, forgiving each other, just as in Christ God forgave you" (Ephesians 4:32).
- When you are lonely
  "Never will I leave you; never will I forsake you" (Hebrews 13:5).
- When times are hard
  "For our light and momentary troubles are achieving for us an eternal glory that far outweighs them all" (2 Corinthians 4:17).
- When you want to give up
  "I can do everything through him who gives me strength" (Philippians 4:13).

- When you are worried

  "Do not be anxious about anything, but in everything, by prayer and petition, with thanksgiving, present your requests to God" (Philippians 4:6).
- When you mess up big-time

  "One thing I do: Forgetting what is behind and straining toward what is ahead, I press on toward the goal to win the prize for which God has called me heavenward in Christ Jesus" (Philippians 3:13–14).
- When you have a need

  "And my God will meet all your needs according to his glorious riches in Christ Jesus" (Philippians 4:19).

These are just a smattering of verses that will equip your child to handle what life throws at him. We can send our children to school to make them smart, but we sow seeds of Scripture to make them wise.

One of my friends, Missy Schrader, told how her grandmother taught her Scripture when she was a preschooler. As with *The New England Primer,* Missy learned one verse for each letter of the alphabet. Because she couldn't write yet, her grandmother asked Missy to draw pictures that reminded her of each verse. When Missy saw a particular picture she had drawn, she remembered the verse that went along with it.

After Missy described her grandmother's memory method, I asked her if she still remembered the verses. Even though twenty-some years had passed, Missy quoted all twenty-six verses without skipping a beat.

Below are the verses she learned. You might want to pull out some paper and crayons and give it a try with your own preschoolers.

A "All we like sheep have gone astray" (Isaiah 53:6 KJV).

B "Be kind to one another"(Ephesians 4:32 RSV).

C "Children, obey your parents; this is the right thing to do" (Ephesians 6:1 TLB).

D "Don't fret and worry—it only leads to harm" (Psalm 37:8 TLB).

E "Every good and perfect gift is from above" (James 1:17 NIV).

F "'Follow me,'" Jesus said, "'and I will make you fishers of men'" (Matthew 4:19 NIV).

G "God is love" (1 John 4:16 NIV).

H "He cares for you" (1 Peter 5:7 NIV).

I "I am the Bread of Life" (John 6:35 TLB).

J "Jesus said, 'Let the little children come to me'" (Matthew 19:14 NIV).

K "Kind words are like honey—enjoyable and healthful" (Proverbs 16:24 TLB).

L "Love one another" (John 13:34 NIV).

M "My sheep listen to my voice; I know them, and they follow me" (John 10:27 NIV).

N "Now is the day of salvation" (2 Corinthians 6:2 NIV).

O "Obey God because you are his children" (1 Peter 1:14 TLB).

P "Pray about everything" (Philippians 4:6 TLB).

Q "Quick, Lord, answer me—for I have prayed" (Psalm 141:1 TLB).

R "Remember your Creator now while you are young" (Ecclesiastes 12:6 TLB).

S "Sing a new song to the Lord" (Psalm 98:1 TLB).

T "Thank God for his Son—his Gift too wonderful for words" (2 Corinthians 9:15 TLB).

U "Underneath are [God's] everlasting arms" (Deuteronomy 33:27 TLB).

V "Visit orphans and widows" (James 1:27 RSV).

W "We love because [God] first loved us" (1 John 4:19 NIV).

X "[Except] a kernel of wheat falls to the ground and dies, it remains only a single seed. But if it dies, it produces many seeds" (John 12:24 NIV).

Y "You must be born again" (John 3:7 NIV).

Z "Zacchaeus, come down immediately. I must stay at your house today" (Luke 19:5 NIV).[2]

Using the alphabet to teach Scripture goes back even further than *The New England Primer*. King Lemuel's mother taught him principles for living using the same method (Proverbs 31). While the young prince sat at his mother's knee, she taught him how to rule his future kingdom (verses 1–9), as well as what to look for in a godly wife (verses 10–31). To make it easy for her son to spot Miss Worth More Than Rubies, his mother began each verse with a letter of the Hebrew alphabet. She made the principles specific and easy for him to remember.

The seeds of Scripture that were planted as a child in author and evangelist Corrie ten Boom gave her the strength she needed to survive the atrocities of a Nazi concentration camp. When Corrie was growing up, each morning her family gathered around the table, and her father read aloud a chapter from the Old Testament. Each evening he read a chapter from the New. Her father told her, "Girl, don't forget that every word you know by heart is a precious tool that [God] can use through you."[3]

Because Corrie had hidden God's Word in her heart, the Nazis couldn't take it away from her. Not only did Scripture help her to bear up under the pain and suffering, but she also became a Bible to those around her. Many turned to Christ because of the seeds that were sown in Corrie as a child.

To some, this emphasis on teaching Scripture might seem like preaching to their children. But I love what Ruth Graham said about her role as a mother and homemaker: "To me, it's the nicest, most rewarding job in the world, second in importance to none, not even preaching." Then she added, "Maybe it is preaching!"[4]

Plant a Garden of Joy

First, plant 5 rows of Peas;

> *Prayer,*
>
> *Perseverance,*
>
> *Politeness,*
>
> *Promptness and*
>
> *Purity.*

Plant 3 rows of Squash:

> *Squash gossip,*
>
> *Squash criticism,*
>
> *And Squash indifference.*

Plant 5 rows of Lettuce:

> *Let us be faithful to duty;*
>
> *Let us be unselfish;*
>
> *Let us be truthful;*

Let us follow Christ;

Let us love one another.

No garden is complete without Turnips:

Turn up for church;

Turn up with a smile;

Turn up with new ideas;

Turn up with determination to make

Everything count as good and worthwhile.

—Author Unknown[5]

Sowing Seeds of Prayer

Hand in hand with sowing seeds of Scripture is sowing seeds of prayer. As Matthew Henry said, "The Bible is a letter God has sent to us; prayer is a letter we send to Him."[6] We learn about God when we read His Word. We become intimately acquainted with God when we spend time in prayer. And when a child comes before the Father's throne, I envision a warm smile spreading across His welcoming face.

In Matthew 19:13, the disciples rebuked parents who brought their children to Jesus for His blessing. I can just imagine the disciples saying, "Get those kids out of here! Can't you see He's busy? Jesus doesn't have time for children. He has more important things to do—and He certainly doesn't have time to pray for your kids!"

But Jesus rebuked the disciples, "Leave the children alone! Allow the little ones to come to Me, and do not forbid or restrain or hinder them, for of such [as these] the kingdom of heaven is composed" (verse 14 AMPLIFIED).

God delights when children come into His presence. What a privilege for us to lead them there.

Just as sowing seeds of Scripture can be as natural as breathing, so can sowing seeds of prayer. First Thessalonians 5:17 says, "Pray continually." Of course we can't spend twenty-four hours a day in prayer. But we can live our lives with an attitude of prayer. When an ambulance goes by, pray with your child about the person inside. When Brooke loses her doll, pray with her to find it. When a test is coming up, pray with your student to do his best.

A few years ago, I taught a Sunday school class of five-year-olds. Prayer time was my favorite segment.

"Do you have anything we need to pray about today?" I asked.

"Pray for my loose tooth, that it'll come out."

"Pray for my tooth, that it'll come in."

"Pray for my cat who is sick, that God will make her better."

"Pray for my dad who lost his job."

"Pray for my dad's friend who went to prison last week because he did bad things."

All the requests held equal importance. The children had not yet learned (from some misinformed adult) that certain requests are too trivial to take to God.

My family began to pray together as soon as Steven could talk. Step by step, we taught him to pray, using the Lord's Prayer as a pattern. We still use that prayer as our guide.

- First, we praise God for who He is.
- Second, we thank God for what He has done.
- Third, we pray for our needs and the needs of others.
- Fourth, we thank Him again for hearing our prayers.

One very important element of prayer that's missing in the above list is confession. Although we stress the importance of confessing our daily shortcomings, Steven prefers to do that in private prayer. I agreed to that plan since I wanted to encourage him to confess, and I didn't want him to fear "getting in trouble" if he confessed aloud. However, I do feel a child should hear Mom and Dad confess their sins as an example that we are all imperfect creatures who make mistakes (with some discretion used in what sins are confessed, of course).

That's our pattern for family prayer, but we shoot up "arrow prayers" to heaven all day long.

Some mothers fear including children in family prayers. "What if I share a prayer request with my child and God says no or doesn't answer the prayer?" Mother asks. "Won't that be a hindrance to my child's faith? Maybe he will think God doesn't really answer prayer."

Steven was almost two years old when my husband and I decided it was time to give him a little brother or sister. Steven was conceived with no problem, so we thought this would be a great opportunity to do a little faith building in our son. We sat him down one night and explained, "Steven, Mommy and Daddy want you to have a little brother or sister. But it's God who blesses parents with children, so we're going to pray that He will bless us with another Jaynes baby."

So every night he prayed, "God, please give Mommy and Daddy another Jaynes baby. Amen."

Well, four years passed, and we had no news of another Jaynes baby to broadcast to our friends and family. I was worried that the situation was going to make God look bad in Steven's eyes.

We had a miniature table and chairs in the kitchen where Steven and I ate lunch together each day. One day Steven looked up and in his sweet little voice said, "Mommy, did you ever think that maybe God only wants you to have one child?"

I quickly shot up one of those arrow prayers and answered, "Yes, I have thought maybe that is the case. If it is, I'm so thankful because He has given me all I ever hoped for in a child wrapped up in one package, *you!*"

Then he turned his little head like a robin and said, "But I think what we ought to do is keep praying until you're too old to have one. Then we'll know that's His answer."

The Lord had spoken to this child and used him to minister to his mother. Steven didn't know how old "too old" was, but he did know that God *could* do anything. If His answer was no, Steven didn't have a problem with that. After all, I'd told him no many times, and he understood that didn't mean, "I don't love you." "No" just meant "No because I said so, and because I know what's best for you."[7]

Sharing family prayer requests with your child can be a growing experience for all concerned, especially the parents.

CHAPTER NINETEEN

$\mathcal{P}$lanting in Season

To every thing there is a season, and a time to every purpose under heaven. . . . A time to plant, and a time to pluck up that which is planted" (Ecclesiastes 3:1–2 KJV). There's a distinct season for planting seeds in our children. It begins the day they are born and lasts about eighteen years.

Almost every night of Steven's life under our roof, we've read a chapter from the Bible and prayed together as a family. We've also listened to audiotapes of Christian stories, such as *Adventures in Odyssey,* by Focus on the Family. As a matter of fact, we've heard those so often I feel as though Mr. Whittaker, one of the main characters, is a part of the family. We started to plant early and still sprinkle a few seeds when we have the opportunity to slip them in.

Take every opportunity to plant good seeds, and when you do, make it as natural as breathing. Teach about Jesus' washing the disciples' feet as you give your child a bath. Talk about how a little bit of sin can grow in our hearts, as you add yeast to dough and watch it rise.

We can plant seeds when we sit around the dinner table, toss a ball, drive to school, wait in checkout lines, serve dinner to the homeless, or keep the church nursery. Seeds of truth are waiting everywhere in life. And seed sowing is not reserved for Sundays. The time to plant is twenty-four hours a day, seven days a week.

Second Corinthians 9:6–8 says (with a little amplification from me) that the more we plant, the more we will reap: "[She] who sows sparingly shall also reap sparingly; and [she] who sows bountifully shall also reap bountifully. Let each one do just as [she] has purposed in [her] heart; not grudgingly [I could be out playing tennis!] or under compulsion [That Sharon Jaynes said I had to memorize Scripture, and we're going to memorize all of Philippians by Tuesday come hail or high water!]; for God loves a cheerful giver. And God is able to make all grace abound to you, that always having all sufficiency in everything, you may have an abundance for every good deed" (NASB).

God loves a cheerful giver—and so do our kids. Communicating our faith shouldn't be drudgery and compartmentalized as "religion." It should be natural and, dare I say, fun.

I remember one day when I was seventeen. I was sitting in our Christian coffeehouse, which was packed with high school students gathered for a weekly Bible study. We had just finished singing praise songs when our study leader became really serious, lowered his voice, and posed the question, "Who came here tonight to have . . . fun?"

My hand was the first to shoot up! As a matter of fact, it was the only one to shoot up. I looked around. Everyone was staring at me as if I had a neon sign blinking over my head that read, "Heathen! Heathen!"

"Wrong answer?" I asked, as I lowered my hand in embarrassment.

With a tsk-tsk look on his sullen face, the leader, who was just a few years my senior, went on to preach his lesson. "We are *not* gathered in this place to have fun. We are here to learn, to study God's Word, to become mature Christians."

But what that twit (excuse me) didn't understand, as he continued to shame me in front of my peers, was that studying the Bible, discovering answers to the mysteries of creation, seeing Jesus Christ revealed in the Old Testament, uncovering the truths that can set you free—that's fun! The Bible is a treasure hunt. It's a love story, a murder mystery, a whodunit. It was exciting to me when I was seventeen, and it's still exciting to me today.

Many years have passed since that embarrassing night at the coffee-house, but I've tried to teach Steven that being a Christian and having fun aren't contradictory. Studying God's Word isn't drudgery. It's exciting! And I hope, if Steven ever finds himself in a roomful of his peers at a Bible study, and the teacher says, "OK, who came here tonight to have fun?" that Steven's hand will be the first to shoot up.

Watching Out for Weeds

After we built our home in 1986, we hauled in truckloads of rich topsoil and spread it over our rocky ground. Then we planted thousands of tiny fescue grass seeds. After several weeks of watering, slender blades of green began to push their way through the dirt in search of the sun-light. Within six weeks, our yard was a carpet of luscious grass that beck-oned us to kick off our shoes and walk barefoot.

The following spring, I noticed a few unwelcome visitors in my prize lawn: dandelions, crabgrass, and ground ivy.

"Steve," I asked, "where did those weeds come from? We surely didn't plant them!"

"The weeds come from seeds that blow in from other places. Mostly from our neighbors' yards," he answered.

After the grass came up that spring, all the green blended in nicely, and we hardly noticed the weeds. However, the next spring, we had more weeds and less grass. By the fourth spring, we knew that if we didn't ap-ply some sort of weed control, soon we would have a yardful of weeds and no grass at all.

When a newborn baby comes bounding into the world, that help-less bundle of joy is so easy to love, coddle, nurture, and protect. We plant good seeds in our children's minds, bodies, and souls. But all too soon, weeds begin to blow in from outside sources, and, if we aren't careful, the fertile soil of youth can be overrun with life-choking weeds.

Webster defines a weed as "any plant growing where it is not desired, especially a wild plant growing in ground under cultivation." Our child's mind, the field under cultivation, is like an incredible computer. Ac-cording to authors Dick Gilling and Robin Brightwell, "The brain has one trillion nerve cells and one thousand times that many neuron connec-tors that enable it to absorb 100 million messages every second."[1] Every second a child experiences a sight, sound, touch, taste, or smell, that's processed for later use. Every second he is receiving messages from somewhere, someone, or something.

Unfortunately, in our society, many times that someone or something is the media. Movies, TV, music, the Internet, and video games glorify sex, violence, and drugs. Children as young as two are spending an average of 16 to 17 hours in front of the television every week, according to a study published in the January 1999 edition of the *American Academy of Pediatrics.* The same study showed that teenagers, who combine television viewing with playing video games, spend 35 to 55 hours per week in front of the television.[2]

Much Top 40 music glamorizes rape, illicit sex, murder, and drugs. Andrew Fletcher, the great Scottish patriot, wrote in 1703, "You write the laws, let me write the music, and I will rule your country."[3] Advertising agencies have known the power of music all along—that's why they use jingles, slogans set to music. A parent knows it's not uncommon to hear little children singing jingles from television ads.

Magazines targeted toward teens are also full of life-choking weeds. In April 2000 I browsed through the magazine aisle to see what girls were reading. Here are a few article titles from publications geared toward teen girls: "What You Think About Sex: Who Does What, Where, and Why"; "Bad Boys, Wild Women, and Kisses Guys Love!" The following is an excerpt about prom night from *Seventeen* magazine (targeting thirteen-year-olds):

> To shave or not to shave: That was the question. This, after all, was my senior prom, the culmination of my high school social career. . . . Oh, sure, I had already bought the frilly new underwear and bra, but I could always convince myself that they were just for "good luck.". . . But the closely shaved legs? There was only one reason to shave them before I went out the door that night—because someone might feel them.[4]

Here are some statistics you should know:

- By the time a child graduates from high school, he will have seen 18,000 murders on TV.[5] According to a national poll conducted by Children Now, 62 percent of kids ages 10 to16 said that sex on TV influences children to engage in sex when they are too young.[6]
- Eighty-nine percent of all sex on TV occurs outside of marriage.[7]

- Every week the average American child between the ages of 2 and 11 years watches 1,197 minutes of TV and spends 39 minutes in conversation with his or her parents.[8]
- Each year nearly 1 million teenagers in the United States, or approximately 10 percent of all 15- to 19-year-old females, become pregnant.[9]
- One-third of these teenage pregnancies end in abortion, while another 14 percent miscarry.[10]
- The number of videos rented daily in the U.S. is 6 million, while the number of library items checked out daily is 3 million.[11]
- During the four hours of Saturday morning cartoons, more than two hundred ads for junk food are shown.[12]
- Twenty-five percent of teenagers ages 13 to 17 can name the city in which the U.S. Constitution was written (Philadelphia); 75 percent know where to find the zip code 90210 (Beverly Hills, as in the *Beverly Hills 90210* TV show).[13]
- Twelve million Americans contract a sexually-transmitted disease of one kind or another every year. At least 3 million of those are teenagers, and perhaps as many as 7 million are in their twenties.[14]

Considering how prolific weeds can be, as blessed moms we dare not grow weary of weeding. Remember, we—and our children—are a culmination of all that has gone into our minds, and we can change what we are by changing the input. Paul said it this way, "Do not conform any longer to the pattern of this world, but be transformed by the renewing of your mind" (Romans 12:2). So weed on! And remember, there is a season for planting and weeding, but it passes quickly.

Harvesting the Fields

One summer I planted five packages of zinnia seeds. I tilled the soil in a little plot of ground, gently nudged the itty-bitty slivers into the earth, and lovingly patted the dirt back in place. Just as the directions on the package instructed, I watered, fertilized, and waited. Four weeks later, little green shoots peeped up from the ground.

But then the painters came and trounced across the flower bed. A few days later, heavy rains came, and then my dog, Ginger, had a notion to dig in one corner of the plot.

In the end, two of the seeds sprouted, took root, and produced four-foot bushes of fuchsia, yellow, and orange zinnias that provided cuttings for the entire summer.

Moms, when it comes to sowing seeds in your children's lives, you may follow the instructions on the package, but the end result isn't up to you. Take, for instance, Susan and Stan, who grew up in the same house, with the same parents, and with the same seeds sown in their lives. Jesus Christ became Susan's cornerstone, the most important person in her life. Her deepest desire was to please Him, obey Him, and develop into the godly woman He desired her to be.

On the other hand, Jesus Christ became Stan's chief stumbling block. He rebelled against God and now lives a life of self-centered pleasure seeking that focuses on money and status.

Two children. One household. Their mother laments, "Where did I go wrong?" My question to her is, "What about the other child? Where did you go right?"

Paul's words to the Corinthians help to give us perspective when we feel fearful about how our "garden" will grow: "Neither he who plants nor he who waters is anything, but only God, who makes things grow. The man [mom] who plants and the man [mom] who waters have one purpose, and each will be rewarded according to his [her] own labor" (1 Corinthians 3:7– 8). We are also reminded by Solomon to keep on planting even if we aren't seeing any fruit. "Sow your seed in the morning, and do not be idle in the evening, for you do not know whether morning or evening sowing will succeed, or whether both of them alike will be good" (Ecclesiastes 11:6 NASB).

Susanna Wesley taught her children each day from nine until twelve o'clock, and then again from two until five. Their primary text was the Holy Bible. Susanna sowed seeds into her children's lives; however, she understood that only God could cause those seeds to grow. To Sukey, one of her children, she wrote:

> You have learned some prayers, your creed, and catechism. But, Sukey, it is not learning these things by heart, nor saying a few prayers morning and night, that will bring you to heaven; you must understand what you say. . . . I cannot tell if you have ever considered the lost and miserable condition you are in nature. If you have not, it is high time to begin to do it, and I

shall earnestly beseech the Almighty to enlighten your mind . . . that you may be His child by adoption, and an heir of His blessed kingdom here after.[15]

So, too, you can sow seed, but God must grant the growth.

When a person has a job outside the home, she finishes a project, and then, within a couple of weeks, she receives a paycheck as a reward for her good work. However, mothering functions under different rules. We plant, we water, we fertilize, we weed, we prune . . . and then we wait. Sometimes we wait for a very long time.

To those of you with wayward children, I offer these words. "Those who sow in tears will reap with songs of joy. He who goes out weeping, carrying seed to sow, will return with songs of joy, carrying sheaves with him" (Psalm 126:5–6). Don't give up! (We'll talk more about that in section 7.)

Meanwhile, in the next chapter we'll read about a mom who knew all about planting, weeding, and harvesting. Her crop provides hope for all of us.

❖ Have your child read the words to questionable CDs aloud to you. Then let him decide if he thinks those CDs are acceptable.

❖ Turn off the television.

❖ Don't be afraid to say no to movies that "everybody else" is seeing.

❖ Buy a roll of tickets at a party store and give a certain amount to your child per week. Each time the child watches thirty minutes of TV, she turns in a ticket. When the allotted time for the week is used up (when no tickets are left), no more TV.

❖ Give a child ten quarters each week. Have him turn in a quarter for each thirty minutes of TV watched. What he doesn't use, he gets to keep. It will be a great investment.

❖ Read movie reviews.

❖ Don't set guidelines that you aren't willing to follow yourself.

❖ Know your child's friends.

❖ Chaperone parties.

❖ Watch TV with your kids to see what they are viewing. When a questionable scene or dialogue is presented, discuss why it's inappropriate.

❖ Listen to your child with your whole being.

- Have young children draw pictures that remind them of Bible verses and put the pictures in a booklet.

- Tape Bible verses on your child's bathroom mirror.

- Learn Scripture songs with your child.

- Have your adolescent pick out a "life verse." This favorite verse will serve as a guide or theme for her life. Mine is "You will know the truth, and the truth will set you free" (John 8:32).

- Make a list of Bible promises for your child to refer to when he needs a boost.

- Pray as a family every night.

- Write down family prayer requests and then check them off when they are answered.

- Read stories to young children that build godly character.

- Suggest that older children read biographies about godly men and women such as Corrie ten Boom, Amy Carmichael, Ben Carson, and Charles Colson.

- Have a family worship time together after a meal.

- Share with your child what the Lord is teaching you in your own quiet time or Bible study.

CHAPTER TWENTY

Sonya Carson:
A Seed-Sowing Mom

*F*rom the time Ben Carson was eight years old, he'd dreamed of becoming a missionary doctor and traveling to primitive villages around the world. Unfortunately, only smart kids were accepted in medical school, and he was at the bottom of his fifth-grade class. Ben's future looked pretty bleak, but he had a mother who was a seed sower.

Sonya Copeland was born in Tennessee to a family of twenty-four children. She never advanced past the third grade. Eager to escape her dreary home life, at thirteen she married Robert Carson, a twenty-eight-year-old man (who already had five children and a wife). In the 1940s the couple moved to Detroit, where Robert worked in an automobile factory. During that time, she had two sons, Curtis, born in 1949, and Ben, born in 1951.

When Ben was eight years old, his father left and never returned. Ben said it was the saddest day of his life. "My shattered life was left in the hands of one amazing woman, my mother, Sonya Carson. Mother pulled off a miracle just battling through life on her own. Yet she still found time to help turn a miracle in mine."[1]

After hearing a missionary doctor's tales in a church service, Ben told his mother he wanted to be a doctor. She said to him, "Bennie, listen to me. If you ask the Lord for something and believe, He will do it, then it'll happen."[2]

But Ben's life seemed to be on a downward spiral. He was failing school. So Sonya decided to pull some weeds and plant some seeds. She came home from work one day and told Ben he had to memorize all his multiplication tables. Of course, he said that was impossible. But Sonya assured him that she would help—and, besides, he couldn't play outside after school until he had them all memorized. Well, the impossible happened, and Ben learned his tables. Not only that, but he also moved from the bottom of his math class to the top.

Another day, Sonya came into the room where Ben and Curtis were watching TV. She snapped off the television in the middle of a program and announced that the boys were watching too much TV. The new house rule was two shows per week. From then on, they had to go to the library and read two books every week. At the end of the week, they had to do a book report. She also made them read the book of Proverbs aloud to her and then explain what they had read.

With academics well under way, Ben had one other area of his life that needed to be brought under control—his temper. At fifteen, he sprang into a fit of rage and stabbed one of his best friends. Fortunately, the knife hit the boy's large belt buckle, saving his life. Horrified at what he had almost done, Ben ran to the bathroom and prayed for two hours for God to deliver him from his temper.

His mother had sown seeds of prayer, and they popped their heads out of the soil that day. "Lord," he prayed, "You've got to take this temper from me. If You don't, I'll never be free from it. You've promised that if we come to You, ask something in faith, You'll do it. I believe that You can change me."[3] That day, God delivered Ben Carson from his volatile temper.

Ben went on to earn a scholarship to Yale University. He then attended medical school at the University of Michigan. Today he is the director of pediatric neurosurgery at Johns Hopkins Children's Center and is world-renowned for some of his miraculous surgeries.

Ben said:

The big difference between people who succeed and people who don't is not that the ones who were successful don't have barriers and obstacles. Everyone has barriers and obstacles. If you look at them as fences that don't allow you to advance, then you're going to be a failure. If you look at them as hurdles that strengthen you each time you go over one, then you're going to be a success.[4]

Ben had someone helping him over those hurdles—a blessed mother who listened to his dreams, encouraged him forward, built self-esteem, and sowed seeds of love, learning, and faith in God. Today, both boys—Curtis, an engineer, and Ben, a doctor—rise up and call her blessed.

BE CAREFUL WHAT YOU SOW

Every plant has little seeds
That make others of its kind.
Apple seeds make apple trees
And they'll do it every time.

Seeds make flowers, shrubs, and trees.
Seeds make ferns, vines, and weeds.
What you plant is what you grow.
So be careful what you sow.
                        —Author Unknown

Preacher G. Campbell Morgan had four sons who became ministers of the Gospel. Someone asked one of the sons which of the four was the best preacher. He glanced over at his father and answered, "Why, it's Mother!"

My mother had a slender, small body, but a large heart—a heart so large that everybody's joys found welcome in it, and hospitable accommodation.

—Mark Twain

SECTION SIX

Be an
Example
Setter

CHAPTER TWENTY-ONE

Someone's Watching You

I saw you at the grocery store today. Oh, you didn't see me. You wouldn't have known me anyway—for I am a stranger to you. But there you were in your slacks and T-shirt, pushing your little girl in the cart, groceries piled around her. You went down the aisle choosing the items on your carefully planned list. (I bet you're having to watch your budget.) I stopped at the other end of the aisle, and, without your awareness, I watched you.

You chatted back and forth with your little one and then impetuously reached over and placed a light kiss of affection upon her little precious cheek.

Quietly I lifted my heart to the Lord and thanked Him for you and asked Him to bless you.

I left you then and continued my own shopping, only to see you again down the next aisle. This time your long, lovely hair was tied in a ponytail, and you wore neat shorts and sandals. Your little boy sat in the top of the cart with his older brother holding down the bottom rack. As you rushed down the aisle, I heard you tell them they could set up the swimming pool on the deck when you got home if they promised to be good.

Again you were unaware you were being watched. But I quietly observed and again lifted you and your family to the Lord.

No, you don't know me—neither do I know you, but I love you and admire and respect what you are doing. For you see, I am an older woman. My years of living your lifestyle have long since passed. In fact, I have grandchildren the ages of your children. I do remember those years of never-ending demands—children, husband, housework, all the things that now consume your every waking moment. I also remember struggling with the feelings of uselessness, the moments of wondering if anyone ever appreciated my many sacrifices, or even noticed.

I watched you today and you did not know . . . but guess who else is watching. If watching you gave me warm fuzzies, just imagine how the Lord must feel! Oh, my dear lady, God loves you so much! How you warm His heart.

I think He would say to you, "My child, my beloved daughter, you are so precious to me. I love you so deeply that I have entrusted to you my greatest responsibility and honor of discipleship: that of being a mother. You are the pastor of a 'great,' although small, congregation. I have placed my dearest possessions, my little babes, into your hands. Care not if those around you understand or appreciate . . . only look up to Me. I am always and forever watching over you, as you tenderly and lovingly watch over them. Be not discouraged, for I am with you."

And from me to you—thank you. You are paving the way, by your example, for a new generation with morals and values that have long been displaced and forgotten. You are our hope for tomorrow . . . our shining star on the horizon.

You may see your task as mundane drudgery at times, but I see you mothers as the warriors on the battlefront—as were Sarah, Hannah, Esther, Mary, Martha—God's chosen handmaidens. I see you as saints![1]

Everything I've written thus far hinges on this one pivotal point: No matter what we say to our children, no matter what values we attempt to instill in their hearts, nothing speaks louder than our actions. We can plant the seeds with our talk, but they will not take root unless they match our walk. A mother whose children rise up and call her blessed is an example setter who demonstrates love, joy, peace, patience, kindness, goodness, faithfulness, gentleness, and self-control in her own life. Children are looking for an example setter who has integrity.

The Blind Leading the Blind

Jesus says in Luke 6:39–40, "Can a blind man lead a blind man? Will they not both fall into a pit? A student is not above his teacher, but everyone who is fully trained will be like his teacher." Teaching our children moral behavior but setting them a poor example is like holding out food in one hand and poison in the other.

In the *Charlotte Observer,* one young teen wrote in to a health question-and-answer column. "My parents are always telling me not to smoke or drink. But they do both. When I point that out, they just say they know best and to listen to what they say. How can I tell them that their behavior is important too?"

The columnists wrote back:

Your parents are probably hoping (and praying) that what they say will carry more weight than what they do. Sorry, it just doesn't work that way. A recent study proved that point. The study published in the September 1999 issue of *The Journal of Health and Social Behavior* found that—just as you thought—teens are more likely to do as parents do and not as they say. Researchers studied 330 teens and their parents for five years. They found that parents who smoked cigarettes, drank too much alcohol, didn't exercise, ate poor diets, and didn't get enough sleep, were more likely to have teens with the same bad habits.[2]

It's another case of what-you-do-speaks-so-loudly-that-I-can't-hear-what-you-say. Our children are watching more than they are listening. They may doubt what you say, but they will believe what you do. Leo B. Blessing (I love that name!) once said, "The foundation of character is built not by lecture, but by bricks of good example, laid day after day."[3]

We may never know the full impact of our actions. Even when we don't realize it, someone's watching. Listen to what one boy had to say about his mother:

When you thought I wasn't looking, I saw you hang my first painting on the refrigerator, and I wanted to paint another one.

When you thought I wasn't looking, I saw you make my favorite cake just for me, and I knew that little things are special things.

When you thought I wasn't looking, I heard you say a prayer, and I believed there is a God I could always talk to.

When you thought I wasn't looking, I felt you kiss me good night, and I felt loved.

When you thought I wasn't looking, I saw tears come from your eyes, and I learned that sometimes things hurt, but it's all right to cry.

When you thought I wasn't looking, I saw that you cared, and I wanted to be everything that I could be.

When you thought I wasn't looking, I looked . . . and wanted to say thanks for all the things I saw when you thought I wasn't looking.[4]

He rose up and called his mother blessed!

Someone's Listening to You

One day at a women's conference I was speaking about giving the gift of encouragement with the words we say. I wore two small cordless microphones clipped to my shirt. One was to project my voice. The other was to record the message so that cassettes could be purchased later. After I finished, the coordinator for the event remarked to the audience, "Can you imagine what it would be like to wear one of these little recording microphones for twenty-four hours?" Every woman in the room laughed. It was kind of a nervous laugh.

The truth is, all of our homes are bugged, as this anonymous piece suggests:

In our homes, there are two microphones per child—one in each ear. These highly sensitive instruments pick up the table prayers, the songs sung, ordinary conversation, and all types of language. These all-hearing microphones transmit all they hear to highly impressionable minds. The sounds then become vocabulary of the child and his basis for action.[5]

Maybe wearing a recording microphone for a few days wouldn't be a bad idea, especially if we played back what we said. What we would hear on the tape is what we will eventually hear coming from our kids.

Listen to your little girl as she plays with her baby dolls. What tone of voice does she use? Is she reprimanding, instructing, or lovingly cuddling them?

My radio partner at The Proverbs 31 Ministry, Lysa TerKeurst, has three little girls. When Hope and Ashley were three and four years old, one of their favorite "let's pretend" games was talking on the phone. Hope pretended she was I, and Ashley was her mom. Boy, were we convicted about how much time we spent on the phone!

Our children also listen to how we treat others. When we show respect and courtesy, those qualities become contagious. When Steven was in elementary school, I taught him to say, "Thank you for having me," when he left a friend's house, and, "Thank you for coming," when a friend left his. Pretty soon all the rambunctious boys in the neighborhood were saying, "Thank you for having me," as they slipped on their muddy sneakers at the door. And Steven replied, "Thank you for coming." This friendly exchange was music to my ears.

I'll never forget the day I was standing near the third-base line at a softball game for third graders. A little guy rounded the bases, and when he passed the third baseman from the opposing team, he said, "'Scuse me." Someone had done a good job with manners—but the kid hadn't yet realized that everything you learned about manners is thrown out the window when it comes to sports!

If we want our children to say "please" and "thank you," they need to hear it from us. "John, would you please take out the garbage?" sounds so much better than "John, take out the garbage." "Sally, thanks so much for making your bed today" isn't that hard to say, either. Our kids listen to how we speak to the waitress, to the bag boy at the grocery store, and to our husbands.

Mother Teresa said, "Kind words are easy to speak, but their echoes are truly endless."

Moms, we're setting an example, good or bad, positive or negative. We're teaching by the way we live our lives, whether we realize it or not. Every day, in every way, our children are becoming what they see in us.

Children Learn What They Live

If a child lives with criticism, he learns to condemn.

If a child lives with hostility, he learns to fight.

If a child lives with ridicule, he learns to be shy.

If a child lives with shame, he learns to feel guilty.

If a child lives with tolerance, he learns to be patient.

If a child lives with encouragement, he learns confidence.

If a child lives with praise, he learns to appreciate.

If a child lives with fairness, he learns justice.

If a child lives with security, he learns to have faith.

If a child lives with approval, he learns to like himself.

If a child lives with acceptance and friendship, he learns to find love in
the world.

—Dorothy Nolte [6]

Someone's Reading You

Charles Swindoll tells the story of four scholars who were arguing over
Bible translations. One said he preferred the King James Version because
of its eloquent old English, another preferred the *American Standard* because of its literalism, and a third preferred the way the *Moffatt* translation captured the reader's attention. After giving the issue considerable
thought, the fourth scholar admitted, "I have personally preferred my
mother's translation." The other scholars chuckled, but he explained, "She
translated each page of the Bible into life. It is the most convincing translation I ever saw."[7]

You've probably heard people say, "My life is an open book." As a
blessed mother who is an example setter, your life *is* an open book, and
your children are reading from every page. They are finding answers to
many of life's questions: "How, as a wife, am I supposed to love and hon-
or my husband?" "How am I supposed to spend my money?" "How
should a Christian act?"

And our children are reading the pages of our lives to draw conclusions about what God is like. Think back to your own childhood. How
did you perceive God? In your eyes, was He a harsh taskmaster who sat
in the clouds, looking down with disapproval every time you made a mistake? Did He carry a big stick, ready to whip you into shape? Did He keep
a big score book in which He made notations when you did something
bad and gave you red check marks when you did something good? Or
did you see Him as a loving father with children clamoring around His
feet and climbing into His welcoming lap? Did you see Him as a daddy

who tucked in His children at night and listened to them talk about anything and everything? Did you see Him as being not mad but hurt when you made a mistake?

As the authors of *The Parent Factor* say, "Whether they have been loving or aloof, kind or harsh, supportive or neglectful, parents have played a major role with forming your view of God. . . . The result can be wonderful or tragic."[8]

Forgiveness Looks Like . . .

Let's take forgiveness, for example. We portray to our children what God's forgiveness is like. Oh, you might have noticed, mothers have ample opportunity to practice the fine art of forgiveness. As we do, we paint a picture of God's grace on the canvas of our children's minds.

Corrie ten Boom was a woman who had much to forgive. She had endured a concentration camp during World War II and then traveled around the world telling how the Lord sustained her. She was often heard to say, "When we confess our sins, God casts them into the deepest ocean, gone forever. And even though I cannot find a Scripture for it, I believe God then places a sign out there that says, 'No fishing allowed.'"[9]

But one day, after she had talked to a crowd of people about God's forgiveness, she saw a man walking toward her. He had been a guard in Ravensbruck, the death camp where she and her sister had been imprisoned. Images of skulls and skeletons, the pathetic piles of dresses and shoes whose owners had been killed, the shame of walking naked past the guards, her frail sister with sharp ribs beneath a parchment of skin marched through Corrie's mind.

The man approached her and said, "A fine message, Fräulein! How good it is to know that, as you say, all our sins are at the bottom of the sea! You mentioned Ravensbruck in your talk. I was a guard there."

Corrie fumbled in her pocketbook, trying not to make eye contact with this man, who had been one of the cruelest of her captors.

"But since that time," he went on, "I have become a Christian. I know that God has forgiven me for the cruel things I did there, but I would like to hear it from your lips as well, Fräulein." He stuck out his hand and said, "Will you forgive me?'

Corrie wasn't sure how long she stood frozen in place. To her, it seemed hours. She wrestled with the most difficult thing she'd ever had to do. With an act of the will, not the emotions, she prayed, *Jesus help me,* and lifted her hand to his. As she did, a current started in her shoulder, raced down her arm, and sprang into their joined hands. "I forgive you, brother!" she cried. "With all my heart."[10]

That, my friend, is forgiveness. As a mother, I must reflect God's forgiving nature back to my child. I've failed so many times in this area. "After all," I've reasoned, "if I let him forget what he has done, he may do it again." So for a time I kept a running list of Steven's wrongs. When I doubted whether he was telling the truth in a certain situation, he would get angry with me. Then I'd pull out my arsenal. "Well, why should I trust you? Remember when you . . . And then there was the time you . . . How is this different?"

After one such stroll down the lane of *This Is Your Life,* with all the mistakes highlighted, Steven just walked out of the room. Later, he told my husband, "I hate it when Mom keeps bringing up all the bad things I've done. If she forgave me, why does she keep bringing it back up?"

When Steve told me of Steven's comment, I cried, thinking how unlike Christ I was toward my son. Later, I asked for Steven to forgive *me.*

Are there certain behaviors you have trouble forgiving your child for? This may not be as difficult with little children, but as they become older and the offenses are graver, letting go and forgiving becomes more of a challenge.

If you have offered the words "I forgive you" but haven't truly done so in your heart, write the wrong you can't let go of on a piece of paper, put it in a paper bag, and burn it in the fireplace. As you see the paper disappear into ashes, visualize it as a sacrifice offered up to God. God will take that forgiveness as a fragrant aroma. Now, when you think about it again, say to yourself, "Oh yeah, I gave that to God already."

A Christian Looks Like . . .

Our children also read the pages of our lives to see what a Christian looks like.

Once a self-righteous, boastful Sunday school teacher was preaching to his class on the importance of exemplary living. With his head held high and chest thrust out, he strutted back and forth across the room. He asked, "Now, children, why do people call me a Christian?"

After a moment of silence, a boy raised his hand.

"Yes?" asked the teacher.

"Probably because they don't know you very well," responded the boy.[11]

The children had read the pages of the teacher's life, and he had come up wanting.

> *You are writing a gospel,*
> *A chapter each day.*
> *By deeds that you do,*
> *By words that you say.*
>
> *Men [children] read what you write,*
> *Whether faithless or true.*
> *Say! What is the gospel*
> *According to you?*
>
> —Author Unknown[12]

*L*ife: A Team Sport

Over the years, my son has had various track coaches, and each coach seems to have a different philosophy about how to train runners. One coach knew all about running—the moves, the stretches, the sprints, the posture, the diet. He told the boys what to do and sent them out on the field to do it. Another coach knew the same information. But he told them what to do and then ran out on the field to do it with them. Which coach do you think gained the most respect? Which coach do you think had the strongest loyalty from the runners?

Our kids need to know that their families are on the same team. They watch to see if the parents cooperate with each other or compete against each other. Zig Ziglar notes that the most critical step to raising positive kids is the relationship between Mom and Dad.

If the child grows up seeing mom and dad showing little respect and kindness toward each other and often engaging in verbal—if not physical—conflict, the child slowly but surely sees that marriage is a battle ground and that the family is not something to enjoy, but something to tolerate—and leave as soon as possible.[13]

If a child hears his mother belittle Dad, it destroys respect and makes the child feel insecure, realizing that the family is at risk of falling apart.

When I was growing up, I didn't feel that my parents were on the same team. They argued a lot in front of my brother and me. I can still remember the fear and uncertainty I felt during my growing-up years. Internally I was living on an earthquake fault line, never knowing when the "big one" was going to hit. There were many big ones.

Moms, please hear me: Fighting in front of your children can leave scars that last a lifetime. Coaxing children to choose sides in their parents' battles tears tender hearts apart. Let's make home where the heart is —where the family pulls for and encourages players—not where the hurt is, as parents compete for a child's affection and loyalty.

Children also need to know that, as a coach, Mom is consistent on the field and off. Dr. Joe White says that "kids are born with big baloney detectors installed like radar in their eyes and ears."[14] They are watching and listening to follow the coach's example. Little eyes watch to see if Mom barks out orders all day long. They watch when she puts back the grocery cart where it belongs. They watch when she speeds through the neighborhood, even if the posted sign says 25 mph.

I was amazed when my son obtained his driver's permit, and I saw how he slung the car around a corner, cutting it close as he turned into our neighborhood—just as he had seen me do for fifteen years. They will follow the coach's lead, won't they?

CHAPTER TWENTY-TWO

The Fruit Doesn't Fall Far from the Tree

I've often heard the statement "The fruit doesn't fall far from the tree," meaning that a child will be like his parent. And I've noticed that this expression generally is used sarcastically, in negative situations. In Galatians 5:22–23, Paul tells us that the fruit of the Spirit is love, joy, peace, patience, kindness, goodness, faithfulness, gentleness, and self-control. Now, if we are a tree with that kind of fruit, then the fruit falling not far from the tree is something to smile about.

What kind of fruit tree do we want to be? What kind of example do we want to set? An example setter cultivates the fruit of the Spirit in her own life. Let's look at the fruit that God deems paramount and see how we can set godly examples for our children. At the end of each quality, I've listed a few ideas to sweeten the fruit.

Love

The film *Chariots of Fire* depicts two incredible runners who represented Great Britain in the 1924 Olympics: Eric Liddle and Harold

Abrahams. Abrahams, a Jewish young man, ran by compulsion. He felt he had to win to fight what he perceived as anti-Semitic views held at his alma mater, Cambridge University. He hired a personal trainer and adopted the attitude that "winning is everything." He said, "I don't run to take a beating. If I can't win, I won't run." He admitted, "I am forever in pursuit, and I don't even know what it is I am chasing."

Eric Liddle, on the other hand, knew exactly what he was pursuing. He ran for God's glory. He said, "God made me fast. When I run, I feel His pleasure. To win is to honor Him."

Harold ran because he had to. Eric ran because he loved to. Both won Olympic medals, but only one felt fulfilled.

We can set that same example, serving God not because we have to but because we love Him. Phillips Brooks said, "Duty makes us do things well, but love makes us do things beautifully."[1]

- Read 1 Corinthians 13 to your child and have him or her write a paraphrase that fits his or her own life. For example: "If I help with the children's nursery on Sunday, but beat my sister on Monday, I am just a big bully."
- Make John 3:16 the first verse your child memorizes.
- Talk about a time when you really felt loved.
- Have your child tell you a time when he or she really felt loved.
- Watch *Chariots of Fire* and talk about the difference between the two principal characters.

*J*oy

When my husband and I purchased a diamond for my tenth-anniversary ring, I noticed that the jeweler placed the sparkling stones on black velvet. The diamonds were beautiful by themselves, but when he nestled them against the dark background, their brilliance shone much brighter.

What a beautiful picture of joy. As we go through dark times, that's when our joy can sparkle the brightest. We moms have the opportunity to be examples of joy by allowing our children to walk through dark times with us—not to burden them unduly but to let them see us sparkle in the darkness.

So many children say, "I'd be happy. . .

. . . if I had a best friend."
. . . if I'd get a Barbie jeep for Christmas."
. . . if I'd get invited to Becky's sleepover."
. . . if I could date Bob the quarterback."
. . . if I could be Bob the quarterback."

Where do kids get the crazy idea that they will have true joy only if certain conditions are met? Could it be they hear their parents say, "I'd be happy . . .

. . . if I could have a maid."
. . . if I'd get a $10,000 raise."
. . . if I could have a bigger house."
. . . if my husband would just treat me the way I want to be treated."
. . . if my child would just do what I ask."

We need to realize and teach our children that happiness and joy are two different things and then model that in our lives.

• Happiness comes from without. Joy comes from within.
• Joy isn't dependent on circumstances but on God's unconditional love for us.
• Joy isn't based on getting what you want but wanting what you have.
• Joy isn't formed by our accomplishments but by what Christ has accomplished for us.

Try these activities with your child:

• Read Philippians aloud and have your child clap each time Paul uses the word "joy" or "rejoice."
• Have your child act out Psalms 146–50.
• Sprinkle some white glitter on a piece of white paper and some on a piece of black paper. Ask your child which shows up better. Explain that joy shows up better during dark times in our lives.

- Read Hebrews 12:2 and ask your child how Jesus could have joy when He knew He was going to die on the cross.
- Read *The Hiding Place,* by Corrie ten Boom. Especially note how Corrie thanked God for the lice in her prison unit because they kept the guard away so that she could share the Gospel.

*P*eace

"Mommy, Mommy, I'm afraid of the dark!" What parent hasn't heard those words? Children learn at a very early age that all sorts of things in this world can rob us of peace. But one little girl showed me that she had discovered the secret to staying peaceful.

She was among an eager group of four-year-old children crowded around my feet as I taught their Sunday school lesson. They listened intently while I tried to create a mental image of Jesus and His disciples on the Sea of Galilee during a thunderstorm.

"The winds bleeew and rocked the little boat back and forth, back and forth," I said. "The waves were sooo big, they splashed over the wooden sides and got the men all wet. Then water started to fill up the boat. And do you know what happens when a boat gets full of water?"

"It sinks," they chimed together.

"That's right," I continued with a concerned look on my face. "Also the lightning was sooo bright, it looked like fire in the sky. And the thunder was sooo loud, they could feel it vibrate in their chests."

After painting this picture of impending doom and thinking I would have my pint-sized audience just a little worried about the fate of these men, I asked, "Now, if you were in a tiny boat, caught in a terrible storm like this, would *you* be afraid?"

Then a little girl, confident and unshaken by the scenario, shrugged her shoulders and replied, "Not if Jesus was in the boat with me."

I'll never forget that answer. As her words echoed in my mind, I realized that her response calms all my worries and fears. Just as the storm raged around the disciples, many times the storms of life rage around me. A friend discovers she has cancer; another friend loses his job; a child is born with birth defects. Our boat, rocked by waves of fear, threatens to spill us into the depths of despair without even a life jacket to keep us afloat.

Tell me, would you be afraid?

Not if Jesus was in the boat with me.

And He is. In Hebrews 13:5, God promises, "Never will I leave you; never will I forsake you." That little girl in the Sunday school class had discovered the secret to everlasting peace. I'm glad I was the teacher that day—or was I?[2]

Explore what peace is with your child:

- Read Genesis 26:24; Exodus 14:13–14; and Joshua 1:5–9 and discuss why the men were told not to be afraid.
- Using a concordance, make a list of all the times "do not fear" is mentioned in the Bible.
- When you're going through a difficult time, explain to your child how you can have peace in that situation.
- Ask, "If you drew a picture of peace, what would it look like?"
- Read John 14:27. How is God's peace different from the world's?

*P*atience

I love to walk down the beach and gather beautiful shells. But unattractive oyster shells are not ones I put in my bucket. However, oyster shells are a splendid picture of what patience can do in our lives.

When an irritant, such as a grain of sand, slips inside the oyster's shell, that bit of sand becomes lodged against the oyster's tender skin. The oyster's first reaction is to spit it out. If that doesn't work, the oyster begins to coat it with layers and layers of a substance called nacre. After time, what began as an irritant becomes a lustrous pearl. The pearl is the oyster's God-given response to the irritants that get under its skin.

Patience is learning to make pearls out of situations that get under our skin. It's willingly waiting to fulfill personal desires, wants, and goals and remaining calm when plans are foiled.

Think of the results of impatience we see every day: speeding tickets, sexual promiscuity, consumer debt, unwise impulse buying, high blood pressure, road rage, child abuse . . .

When we're standing in the checkout line and the person in front of us has an item that requires a price check, what kind of face does our child see on us? Experienced any road rage lately? How about those credit card bills? Could we be teaching impatience when we charge to get now and pay for it later?

How does a blessed mother teach patience?

- Have your child save for a large purchase.
- Help your child open a savings account, and show him how you save.
- Show your teen the total cost of a car bought with cash and a car bought on credit.
- Place some oyster shells around the house to remind everyone that jewels are formed with patience.
- Be a patient parent.
- Read James 1:2–4 and talk about how patience is developed.

Kindness

When Steven was fourteen, he traveled on a missions trip to Little Haiti in Miami. He went as an act of kindness and to teach vacation Bible school to the Haitian children. However, he probably learned more about great acts of kindness than the Haitians did. The home in which he stayed had one window-unit air conditioner in the master bedroom. The parents insisted that the team's adult leader sleep in the air-conditioned room while the family slept on the floor in the den. The other bedroom was given to Steven and his friend.

After Steven returned from his ten-day excursion, I took his clothes to the laundry room, expecting ten days of sweat and odor to jump out at me from his bag. Instead, I pulled out clean, neatly folded T-shirts and shorts and spotless paired socks. I pictured Mrs. A.'s loving hands folding those freshly laundered T-shirts and inverting socks while whispering a prayer for my child. She had no washing machine. She had no dryer. But she did have a heartful of kindness. I held his bag in my lap and cried.

Spread a little kindness:

- Volunteer as a family at a local soup kitchen or homeless shelter.
- Allow your teen to go on a missions trip to an impoverished part of the country.
- Write notes or send cards to friends who are hurting. Help your child pick out cards to send to his friends who are having a hard time.
- Encourage your child to invite to your home a schoolmate who always is left out.

• If a person generally is chosen last for a team at school, encourage your child to pick him first.

Goodness

Of all the Christmases Mike Wekall remembers, his seventh stands out from the rest. Mike was the fifth of six Wekall children. As with any child, December ushered in the anticipation of new toys, freshly baked goodies, glittering decorations, and time off from school. But one week before Christmas, Mike's parents called the children into the den.

"Kids, I have some bad news for you," Mr. Wekall said, barely able to look at them. "As you know, things have been pretty tight at work this year. As a matter of fact, we're going to have to file bankruptcy, so we won't have Christmas. I'm sorry. Maybe we can make it up to you next year." Then he walked out of the room.

The children just sat there for a while in silence. Mike thought, *What does he mean, "We won't have Christmas"? Does that mean I've been bad and Santa isn't going to come? And what is bankruptcy?*

Mike was pretty confused, but one thing became perfectly clear on Christmas morning. Christmas had not come to the Wekall house. No presents under a tree, no aroma of roasting turkey in the kitchen.

The family did, however, go off to church that crisp, cold morning. When they arrived at church, all the other children were sporting new clothes and chattering about what they had found under their trees.

"Hey, Mike, what did you get?" one asked.

"Nothin'. We didn't have Christmas at our house. We're having a bankruptcy."

"What's wrong? Have you been too bad to get anything?"

Feeling rather blue, the family of eight went home for a lunch of lima beans and ham hocks. About an hour later, the doorbell rang.

Maybe it's Santa after all, Mike thought as he ran to the door.

Standing in the doorway wasn't Santa but the Bosky family, all ten of them. All eight children had smiles on their faces and two gifts in their hands. Mr. and Mrs. Bosky held a turkey dinner with all the trimmings.

As it turned out, the eight Bosky children had gone home from church and told their parents about how the Wekalls weren't having Christmas this year. Seeing how they had been so richly blessed, the children decided to each pick two of his toys and wrap them up for the Wekalls. Mom and Dad joined in and brought gifts for the parents. Even though Mrs. Bosky had Christmas dinner all choreographed for her own dining room, she gathered up the food in boxes and baskets to share with a family who needed it more.

Mike is now forty years old, but he still gets teary eyed when he tells this story. "It was the best Christmas I've ever had," he told me. "The Spirit of God showed me that Christmas wasn't about getting presents but about giving and caring for others. It's about showing goodness toward other people. Every year I tell this story to someone, because it exemplifies how Christ gave freely of Himself for us."

That's how we exemplify goodness to our children.

I always thought the word *goodness* in Galatians 5:22 meant "being good" or "good behavior." Then I looked up the Greek word, *agathosune,* and found it means "goodness that does good toward other people." It's not so much about *being* good as it is about *doing* good.[3]

Now, a few ways for your family to do some good:

- Ask for the name of a needy family at your church and buy Christmas presents for them.
- Help an elderly person in your neighborhood.
- Sponsor a child for Operation Christmas Child or Project Angel Tree.
- Suggest that a child do chores for a sibling for no reason at all.
- Read the story of the Good Samaritan and discuss what he did to deserve being labeled "good."

Faithfulness

On September 6, 1995, for more than twenty-two minutes, 42,000 baseball fans stood, applauded, and shouted for Cal Ripken at Camden Yards in Baltimore. It was the sound of America applauding not just for a man and his record but for the faithfulness he represented. What did this thirty-five-year-old shortstop do to earn such accolades? He showed up for work. For 2,131 games straight, Cal came to work and gave it all he had. For fourteen seasons, he never once called in sick or decided to "sit this one out."

"Whether your name is Gehrig or Ripken, DiMaggio or Robinson, or that of some youngster who picks up his bat or puts on his glove,"

Cal said, "you are challenged by the game of baseball to do your very best, day in and day out. And that's all I've ever tried to do."

When asked about his impending record-setting playing streak, he was often quoted as saying, "It's not that big of a deal. I'm just doing my job."[4]

Well, Cal, it *is* a big deal. Just look at the divorce rate in this country, and you can see that faithfulness is falling by the wayside. It's a rarity.

Just in case this baseball story is too masculine for some of us moms, another great example of faithfulness is found in one of Jan Karon's characters from her Mitford series. Uncle Billy Watson was an elderly man married to an eccentric schizophrenic named Rose. She was often seen parading around town in her deceased brother's combat boots and a bomber jacket, or in a chenille robe, argyle socks, and a shower cap. But for forty-three years, through all her escapades, Uncle Billy remained faithful.

One day, the leading character in the series, Father Kavanaugh, asked, "Uncle Billy, I don't know how you've lasted with Miss Rose all these years."

"Well, I give 'er my word, don't you know."[5]

"I give 'er my word." Uncle Billy made a promise. It sounds so simple. Let's teach by example how to be a person who is true to her word.

- Don't divorce.
- If you make a promise to your child, don't break it.
- If your child commits to being on a team, don't let him or her quit until the season is over.
- Read about Jonathan and David and see how David was faithful to his promises (1 Samuel 18–20 and 2 Samuel 9).
- If your child starts a project around the house, insist that he complete it.
- Praise your child for following through with a task or project that he didn't particularly enjoy.

Gentleness

I'm always amazed when I see young riders sitting on large horses, controlling them with a tug of the rein or a tap of the heel. The horse is a powerful animal, yet it isn't good for much unless someone can control it.

The word *gentleness* in Galatians 5:23 is the Greek word *prautes,* which suggests a wild horse that has been tamed. Unfortunately, in our modern society, the word *gentleness* connotes being weak. The Greek word means anything but weak. Picture a muscular steed, proudly holding his head, poised to move with speed and power, nostrils flaring but, at the same time, under his master's control. Now, that's a picture of submission to authority.

The same word, *prautes,* is translated "meek" in the King James Version.[6] When Jesus said He was "meek and lowly in heart" (Matthew 11:29), He was saying He was submitted to God. Only when we submit to God will we have power to live victoriously. Meekness isn't weakness; it's power under control. By letting our children see us submit to God, we exemplify true gentleness.

- Read *Black Beauty* with your child and talk about how the horses were of more use when they were tamed.
- Visit a stable and watch riders on their horses. Ask, "Do the horses look weak?"
- Read Matthew 5:5 and discuss what it means that the meek will "inherit the earth."
- Read 1 Peter 3:15–17 in the *New International Version.* How would answering in a gentle manner someone's hostile question about Christ show control? Suppose you answered that person in anger? Which way would be more effective?

Self-Control

Mom is strolling down the toy store aisle when little Johnny spots a Mighty Mac Laser Gun. He wants it, and he wants it now.

"Mom, can I have that Mighty Mac Laser Gun? Everybody has one."

"No, Son. I'm not buying you anything today. We're here to buy a birthday present for Mark."

"Pleeeaaassseee, Mommy."

"No, Johnny. I'm not buying you the gun."

"I want the gun," Johnny screams at the top of his lungs.

"No," Mom calmly replies as she keeps going down the aisle.

At this point, Johnny falls to the floor, kicks his feet in the air, and wails. Other parents turn to stare. The employees don't even notice; they've heard it all before. What does Mom do?

She could give in. After all, she's terribly embarrassed. One hundred shoppers are peeking around the aisles to see Johnny's tantrum, and the gun only costs $4.99. Or she could smile at the gawkers as she leaves little Johnny screaming on the floor.

If she's smart, she'll let him scream. After all, this isn't about a Mighty Mac Laser Gun. It's about your child, who will soon be twelve years old with the self-control to change a television station when objectionable material is shown. It's about a teenage boy who has the self-control to walk away from a beautiful girl who is encouraging a sexual relationship. It's about a college junior who has the self-control to resist when someone pulls out a bag of marijuana at a party.

Self-control begins when we set limits for our children and help them learn to stay within those boundaries. Sometimes we have to tell them no in the hope that they will learn how to say no themselves. It's a hard lesson to teach. Don't be surprised if you're labeled "just plain mean."

Here's what a friend of mine, Cheri Jimenez, had to say about her mean mom:

"I had the meanest mom in the whole wide world. While other kids enjoyed Pop Tarts and Kool-Aid for breakfast, I was made to eat granola and fruit. While other kids traded bologna sandwiches and Little Debbie cakes at lunch, I was lucky if I could pull off a legitimate trade with my icky tuna fish and celery sticks. At dinnertime, my mean mom made us eat what was on our plates and wouldn't cook separate dishes for my brother and me.

"Mom always had to know where we were, and she could track us down in no time flat. She was always checking up on the type of friends we hung out with; I suspect she was a part-time investigator on the side.

"Oh, how my mom loved schedules. She had us hopping from morning till evening. Daily family devotions and Scripture memory were required. I'm embarrassed to admit it, but I believe she even violated some child labor laws. I had to clean my bedroom, the bathroom, dust, vacuum, and do yard work. And can you believe it, I didn't even get paid!

"By the time I was a teenager, my mom had acquired quite the reputation for meanness among my friends. They knew no wild parties were going to happen at my house, and if we wanted to watch a movie, it had to pass my mom's inspection.

"Dating was another area of abuse. My mom scared off plenty of potential boyfriends with her old-fashioned rules and regulations, such as curfews and making the guys meet my parents.

"I grew up to be a healthy, disciplined, hardworking, God-fearing woman, married to a man who appreciates and respects those standards of living. And whom do I have to thank for this? You're right, my mean old mom.

"I'll be starting a family of my own soon, and secretly I'll be tickled when my children call me mean. I thank God for giving me the meanest mother in the whole wide world."

Don't be surprised if your children rise up and call you mean, but later, as in this case, they will rise up and call you blessed.

- If a child throws a temper tantrum in a toy store, don't buy the toy for him.
- Teach a young child to sit in "Big Church" quietly. (Just like Mommy does.)
- Have self-control yourself. Try not to yell at your child. It has as much effect as a police officer yelling at you for speeding instead of calmly writing you a ticket.
- Teach your child not to interrupt when you're speaking with another adult.
- Give age-appropriate allowance for spending money. And don't make "loans." When the money is gone, it's gone.

So there you have it, the fruit we want to fall close to our tree. Lovely, plump, pleasing fruit that would make any parent proud.

CHAPTER TWENTY-THREE

Mary Ruth Diffey: An Example-Setting Mom

Mary Ruth Diffey, one of my good friends, received this gift for her forty-fifth birthday: her eighteen-year-old daughter, Elizabeth, rose up and called her blessed! Here's the letter Elizabeth wrote:

Dear Mom,

As another year of your life has passed, I cannot do anything but feel so very thankful for you. God has richly blessed me by giving me such a wonderful mother and friend in you. I know that we don't get to spend as much time together as you and I both would like, but I hope and pray that you know just how important you are to me. I have tried to organize my thoughts into a list, so here it goes!!

1. I love you, Mom, because you gave me life.
2. I love you, Mom, because you loved me first.
3. I love you, Mom, for showing me God and His grace and love.
4. I love you, Mom, because you are my hero.

5. I love you, Mom, because you are my best friend.

6. I love you, Mom, because you know me like you know yourself.

7. I love you, Mom, because you love me even when I mess up.

8. I love you, Mom, because you tell me the truth even when it hurts.

9. I love you, Mom, because there is never a time you won't listen.

10. I love you, Mom, because you aren't always right.

11. I love you, Mom, when you tell me special things.

12. I love you, Mom, when you get angry at me.

13. I love you, Mom, for working so hard to keep up with our family.

14. I love you, Mom, because I know there is nothing you would not do for me.

15. I love you, Mom, because I see in you the woman God desires for me to be.

16. I love you, Mom, for teaching me the things I need to know to make it in this world.

17. I love you, Mom, for putting up with me through my teenage years.

18. I love you, Mom, when we disagree.

19. I love you, Mom, when we are getting along really well.

20. I love you, Mom, when I see you smile.

21. I love you, Mom, when I hear others talk about how great you are.

22. I love you, Mom, and am so proud to call you my mom.

23. I love you, Mom, because you are so much fun.

24. I love you, Mom, because you make great food . . . even though I don't always eat it all.

25. I love you, Mom, because you care about what is going on in my life.

26. I love you, Mom, because you have shown me what love really is.

27. I love you, Mom, because you have an incredible zest for life.

28. I love you, Mom, because you know what I am going to say even before I say it.

29. I love you, Mom, for never giving up on me.

30. I love you, Mom, because you are beautiful.

31. I love you, Mom, because you are patient.

32. I love you, Mom, because you are gentle and kind.

33. I love you, Mom, because you have the most humble heart and spirit of anyone I know.

34. I love you, Mom, because you always put everyone before yourself.

35. I love you, Mom, because you make me laugh and cry . . . sometimes at the same time.

36. I love you, Mom, because you always forgive me, even when I have been a real jerk.

37. I love you, Mom, for spending time with me.

38. I love you, Mom, for trying so hard to keep track of all my activities.

39. I love you, Mom, for worrying about me when I am not home on time.

40. I love you, Mom, for all you encouraged me to try and do through the years.

41. I love you, Mom, for pretending like it doesn't bother you that I am so busy.

42. I love you, Mom, because even though you don't like how busy I am, you still let me do my own thing.

43. I love you, Mom, for not being too protective, but for letting me grow up and become independent.

44. I love you, Mom, for trusting me to do the right thing.

45. I love you, Mom, for having faith in me . . . even when no one else did.

46. I love you, Mom, for giving me a brother.

47. I love you, Mom, for being a wife that honors God, and a role model of the bride Christ desires me to be.

48. I love you, Mom, because there's no one else on earth I want to be like more than you.

49. I love you, Mom, for the way you make me feel when we are together.

50. I love you, Mom, for providing for my needs.

51. I love you, Mom, for your wisdom and insight.

52. I love you, Mom, for putting up with me every morning when I wake up (or don't wake up) grouchy.

53. I love you, Mom, for your desire to grow closer and closer to Christ.

54. I love you, Mom, because you do not gossip.

55. I love you, Mom, because you are a strong person.

56. I love you, Mom, because you gave me morals and values that I will never forget.

57. I love you, Mom, because you led me to my Lord and Savior, Jesus Christ.

58. I love you, Mom, for your heart that wants nothing but to serve and please God.
59. I love you, Mom, for not acting old.
60. I love you, Mom, for being so cool.
61. I love you, Mom, because there is nothing you would not do to help me succeed and reach my goals.
62. I love you, Mom, for being you.

My prayer on your 45th birthday is nothing more than this: that you would know and feel just how much I think of you and love you. You are the first person that comes to mind when I think of what I want to become in this life. I have loved every minute of life that God has allowed us to spend together and every memory we have made. I pray that He will continue to bless your life daily and that He will give you not only a wonderful year being forty-five, but many wonderful years following that. You don't know just what it means to me to have you in my life. I still need you very much, and I long to spend more and more time with you. I think the world of you, Mary Ruth Granger Diffey, and I am so proud to call you my mother, my teacher, and my very best friend. Friends and acquaintances will come and go, but family lasts forever. I wish you a wonderful birthday today and many happy birthdays to come.

I love you more than you could ever know,
Elizabeth Granger Diffey

LITTLE EYES ARE UPON YOU

There are little eyes upon you,
And they're watching night and day;
There are little ears that quickly
Take in every word you say.

There are little hands all eager
To do anything you do,
And a little one who is dreaming
Of the day she'll be like you.

You are the little darling's idol.
You are the wisest of the wise.
In her mind, about you
No suspicions ever rise.

She believes in you devoutly,
Holds that all you say and do;
She will say and do in her own way
When she's a grown-up like you.

There's a wide-eyed little one,
Who believes you are always right.
And her ears are always open,
And she watches you day and night.

You are setting an example
Every day in all you do,
For the little one who's watching
To grow up and be like you.

   —Author Unknown[1]

Grace was in all her steps,

Heaven in her eye,

In every gesture dignity and love.

—John Milton

SECTION SEVEN

Be
Diligent

CHAPTER TWENTY-FOUR

Don't Give Up

I have a confession to make. At the beginning of this book, I said that I was in labor for twenty-three hours. That's not completely true. It's been more like seventeen years—and I'm not finished yet! Being a mother has been the most fulfilling, frustrating, exciting, exhausting, mind-boggling, hair-raising, thrilling, tiring, stimulating, soul-stirring, delightful, difficult, consuming, laborious, uplifting, inspiring, challenging, captivating, and rewarding job I've ever had.

My son has held my heart, and, as a result, it has been warmed, broken, squeezed, pained, tickled, hugged, and filled to overflowing with love. Over the course of these seventeen years, Steven has pulled on my heartstrings like an angel plucking the strings of a golden harp to fill the heavenlies with beautiful music.

Now, before you envision my son with a halo and wings, you need to know that some days I've felt as though those heartstrings were being plucked by a little devil's pitchfork. I've had times when I felt like throwing up my hands in frustration and saying, "I quit! Is what I'm doing making any difference—to anyone? I want results! Show me results!" Then I think of the bamboo.

Zig Ziglar, in his book *Raising Positive Kids in a Negative World,* tells how the Chinese grow bamboo. First they plant the seeds, then water, and fertilize them. The first year, nothing happens. The second year they continue to water and fertilize the seeds, and still nothing happens. The seed sower continues this process for a third and fourth year with no visual results. Then sometime during the fifth year, in a period of approximately six weeks, the Chinese bamboo grows ninety feet. The question is, did it grow ninety feet in six weeks or did it grow ninety feet in five years? The obvious answer is that it grew ninety feet in five years because, if the grower hadn't applied water and fertilizer every year, no Chinese bamboo would exist.[1]

The mother whose children rise up and call her blessed is diligent. She doesn't give up if she doesn't see immediate results or if times get hard; she doesn't give up when she has to repeat herself time and time again; and she doesn't give up as she compares herself with more "successful" mothers. With the determination of the bamboo farmer, she waters and fertilizes year after year and is determined to give mothering her all.

Just like Steven, who wanted to quit when we were teaching him how to ride his bicycle without training wheels, maybe you've wanted to give up from time to time. Remember how I described him clenching his little jaw and emphatically announcing, "This is not fun. This will never be fun." I am sure as you've read these chapters on how to be a great mom who raises great kids, you've thought about the piles of laundry, the sticky apple juice spilled on the freshly scrubbed linoleum floor, or that long walk down the school hall to the principal's office, and you've thought, *This is not fun; this will never be fun.* But just as Steven eventually learned to ride without training wheels, we can learn to be a blessing to our children. It takes practice and diligence. Is it easy? No. Is it possible? Yes. If motherhood were easy, it wouldn't start with something called "labor"!

"Camel" Mom

Bumps do occur in the road that threaten to throw us off balance and leave us emotionally depleted. That's when I become a "camel" mom. When mothering is running smoothly, filled with pleasant surprises and spontaneous acts of love, I need to store up—just as a camel stores water in his hump—those treasured moments. The hugs, the quickly written notes, the Mother's Day cards all are neatly packed up and preserved in my heart. Then, on the desert days, when I become discouraged, I can pull out one of my treasures to remind myself of why I'm doing this in the first place.

As blessed mothers, we are available Beacons, avid Listeners, loyal Encouragers, Self-Esteem Builders, Seed Sowers, and Example Setters. And, with diligence, we persevere until our offspring sprout up to maturity.

Perseverance means repeating the same life lessons over and over again until the child finally "gets it right." During one of John Wesley's lessons with his mother, his father became frustrated at her repetitive instruction. He exclaimed, "Susanna, why do you tell that lad the same thing for the hundredth time?"

"Because," she answered, "the ninety-ninth time he did not understand."[2] She was diligent.

For the first nine years of Steven's academic career, I reminded him over and over again to write down his assignments. I got tired of repeating myself but was determined to teach him responsibility. I could have said, "OK, just forget it. Make a zero. See if I care." (Actually, I did say that a time or two.) But the truth is, I did care. I cared enough to repeat the instructions over and over until he finally got it. On the days when I wanted to throw up my hands in frustration, I folded them in prayer instead.

Giving Up vs. Taking a Rest

I've come to realize that giving up and taking a rest are not the same thing. We all need a break from time to time. Mothers need time to recharge, refuel, and refresh. When Steven was two years old, some days I would brush quickly past my husband as he came in the door from work. "Hi, honey," I'd say. "I have to take a break." And off I'd go to walk around the mall or the neighborhood for thirty minutes.

One mother with three active boys was playing cops and robbers with them in the backyard after dinner on a summer evening. One of the boys "shot" his mother and yelled, "Bang, you're dead." She slumped to the ground, and when she didn't get up right away, a neighbor ran over to see if she had been hurt in the fall.

As the neighbor bent over her, the overworked mother opened one eye and said, "Shhh. Don't give me away. It's the only chance I get to rest."[3]

When I was on an airplane recently, the flight attendant gave her usual instructions on the use of the oxygen mask. She said, "If you're traveling with young children, place the mask on yourself first, then assist the child." I thought, *That seems a little selfish,* until I realized that if I passed out, I certainly wouldn't be much help to the child sitting next to me.

So, too, moms need to have a break from time to time to take a deep breath. That's not quitting; that's refueling.

The Myth of Supermom

Don't you just detest the mom who seems to have it all together? You know her: Supermom. She is that mythical creature who never yells at her kids, whose house always is spotless, whose children obey quickly and quietly, who prepares three square meals a day that are nutritious and aesthetically pleasing. She's the "successful" mother.

If anything can cause a mother to want to give up, it's comparing herself to this creature who exists only in storybooks. I can assure you that every mother who appears to breeze effortlessly through life has struggles. But some moms put up a good façade of "togetherness." Rather like my husband on his first visit to the ski slopes.

When I taught Steve how to snow ski, I showed him how to turn his skis toward the side of the mountain to slow down. Inevitably he turned too far to the left or right and ended up with his skis pointing up the mountain. He then proceeded to slide down the mountain backwards. After a few trials and lots of error, he discovered that if he just continued turning his skis when he turned—making a complete circle—it would slow him down and he wouldn't end up going downhill backwards. It was a sight to behold, but it worked.

At the end of the day, a woman came up to Steve and asked if he could show her how to make those "beautiful circles." Of course he obliged. She thought he was an expert skier who was doing some form of acrobatics. In actuality, he was going in circles, doing whatever it took to keep from sliding downhill backwards.

When you look around and see other mothers who appear to be mothering better than you, don't be fooled. They are probably doing whatever it takes not to go downhill backwards.

Successful mothers aren't the ones who never have struggles. They are the ones who never give up, despite the struggles.

Calvin Coolidge said:

Nothing in this world can take the place of persistence. Talent will not; nothing is more common than unsuccessful people with talent. Genius will not; unrewarded genius is almost a proverb. Education will not; the world is full of educated derelicts. Persistence and determination alone are omnipotent. The slogan "press on" has solved and always will solve the problems of the human race.[4]

I'd like to add that God is the only One who is omnipotent, but persistence and determination while relying on His power bring great results!

Don't Lose Heart

Galatians 6:9 reminds us, "Let us not lose heart in doing good, for in due time we shall reap if we do not grow weary" (NASB). That's a promise that we all can cling to.

Being a diligent mother reminds me of the story of a world-famous violinist. An admiring fan ran up to him one day and cried, "Mr. Kreisler, I'd give my life to play as you do!" To that he replied, "Madam, I did."[5] Some people treat being a mother like playing a slot machine, putting in as little as possible and hoping to hit the jackpot. But being a mother is a diligent investment of sacrifices that reaps dividends with compounded interest over time.

Susanna Wesley described her diligent attitude this way:

No one can, without renouncing the world, devote twenty years of the prime of their life in hopes of saving the souls of their children, which some women think you can do without much ado. But that was my intention, to give twenty years of my life to it.[6]

A little nine-year-old boy wanted to give up. He desperately wanted to stop taking piano lessons. In hopes of encouraging her son to continue, his mother took him to hear the great concert pianist Ignacy Jan Paderewski. Before the concert began, the boy slipped away from his mother and made his way to the grand Steinway positioned on the stage under the spotlight. He sat down on the piano bench, placed his chubby hands on the keys, and began to bang out the most annoying song known to humanity— "Chopsticks." The indignant crowd began to yell for someone to get the boy off the stage. Behind the curtain, Paderewski heard the commotion. He grabbed his coat, ran out on stage, and reached his arms around the boy to play a beautiful melody to enhance the boy's "Chopsticks." All the while he whispered in the boy's ear, "Don't quit. Keep on playing. Don't stop. Don't quit."[7]

That's how it is with motherhood. Some days our efforts are just about as melodious as "Chopsticks." When you feel that way, imagine your heavenly Father coming up behind you, placing His loving arms around you, and playing a melodious piece to enhance your simple efforts. All the while He is whispering in your ear, "Don't quit. Don't stop. Never quit."

Legend has it that Winston Churchill delivered one of his most famous speeches to a group of graduating college students who were about to embark on the incredible journey of life with all of its challenges. He stood up and said nine powerful words and then sat back down. The words? "Never give up. Never give up. Never give up." That's my charge to you. No matter what, never give up. Be diligent until the end.

CHAPTER TWENTY-FIVE

Don't
Give In

*A*s I watched my son play in a high school basketball game, I saw the boys were whacking each other left and right. I was about to ask the manager to rummage through the football equipment and bring out the helmets and shoulder pads. Even though parents on both sides were yelling, "Foul, foul!" the referee never said a word.

"Steve," I asked my husband, "why are they playing so rough?"

"Because the ref isn't calling any fouls. The guys will play as rough as they can get away with. If he lets them hack each other on the head, arm, and back, they'll do it. If he starts calling fouls, they'll stop."

Sure enough, the next time I watched Steven play, we had a different referee. The boys saw right away that the official wasn't going to let them get away with anything. That night they played a much "nicer" game of ball.

It's the same way with mothering. Our children will play the game of life just as rough as we allow, testing the boundaries on a regular basis. We may tell them the rules, but they want to know if we are woman enough to enforce them. Let's not disappoint them! A mother who has children who rise up and call her blessed is one who is diligent in discipline. She doesn't give up, and she doesn't give in.

A Bit of Divine Love

We've already established that the best book on parenting is the Bible, so let's see what God has to say about discipline. Proverbs 13:24 says, "He who spares the rod hates his son, but he who loves him is careful to discipline him." The Bible depicts discipline as an act of divine love: Proverbs 3:12 says, "The Lord disciplines those he loves."

Looking back at Proverbs 13:24, we see that Solomon mentions the rod. The rod in biblical times was used by shepherds to protect, to guide, and to rescue sheep from harm. (Nothing is more annoying than unruly sheep.) In our home, the rod was a ruler with the words "Fox Run" printed above the numbers. I kept it on top of the refrigerator, and Steven knew if Mom went after the "Fox Run," he was in big trouble. Because I used a neutral object and not my hand, Steven was afraid of the paddle, but he wasn't afraid of me. Nowhere in Scripture are we instructed to administer physical punishment to our children with our hand.

I remember the days when I was a child and paddling was allowed in public school. In my elementary schoolroom, a ruler hung from a nail on the wall. Printed above the numbers were the words "The Board of Education." I didn't like seeing that ominous piece of wood looming ever before me. However, looking back, I recall that we were a very cooperative group of children. Mrs. Morgan had no trouble teaching the class of thirty-some children without the help of a teacher's aide.

I know spanking is a very sensitive subject these days. It seems that you can't pick up a newspaper or turn on the nightly news without seeing how one of God's precious children has been abused and mistreated. It breaks my heart, and I know it breaks God's heart. Because of abusive, emotionally sick adults who are out of control, many people have decided that all forms of corporal punishment are detrimental.

Satan's Twist

Satan isn't very creative. As a matter of fact, he can't create anything at all. Instead, he takes what God made for good and distorts, twists, and corrupts it for evil. For example, God created sex to be a beautiful expression of love between a husband and a wife—two becoming one flesh. Satan has taken this gift and corrupted it with pornographic addictions, sexual perversions, and extramarital affairs. He has done the same with discipline—taken what God intended for good, and twisted it for evil. Physical punishment, as outlined in the Bible, is an effective form of discipline when administered lovingly and with a spirit of instruction and training.

I know how hard it can be to spank a child. I remember my mother saying, "This is going to hurt me more than it's going to hurt you." I didn't believe a word of it back then—not one little bit. But when I became a parent, I heard myself saying those same words. I'm sure that Steven didn't believe me—not one little bit. But many times after I spanked him, I left him in his room to cry, and I went to mine to cry.

One key to effective physical punishment is to follow it quickly with forgiveness and affection. A child needs to know that you still love him even though he disobeyed. Often, after Steven was spanked, he would reach out his arms to me to be held. And I would willingly welcome him into my lap. A child can feel devastated if a parent spanks him and then withholds affection. Children need reassurance that, although what they did was unacceptable, *they* aren't unacceptable, bad, and unworthy of love.

A few spanking guidelines are:

- Never spank a child in anger.
- If you are angry, count to 100 to cool down. If that doesn't work, keep counting.
- Spank a child only on his or her bottom. That's why God put the extra cushion there!
- Never hit a child in the face or any other part of the body.
- Reserve spanking for willful acts of disobedience, not careless, childish mistakes such as spilling milk, soiling clothes, or forgetting homework.
- If spanking is used routinely as a means of punishment, it will lose its effectiveness. Reserve it for serious offenses.
- Spank a child only in private. Never shame him or her in front of other siblings or in public.
- For a spanking to be effective, the child must feel genuinely loved.
- Offer forgiveness quickly and lovingly.

- Don't expect a two-year-old to act like a ten-year-old.
- If you overreact, apologize.
- With all discipline, stress to the child that the behavior was unacceptable, not that the child is unacceptable. For example, rather than saying, "You're a liar, and I don't tolerate a liar," say, "You told a lie, and I don't tolerate lies." Rather than, "You are a bad boy," say, "That was a bad thing you did."
- Spanking should cease when your child is ten to eleven years old. After that, taking away privileges such as TV, time with friends, video games, or the car keys is very effective.
- Use a neutral object such as a paddle or a ruler, not your hand. We've all seen a child flinch when her mother reached out for her. A child should know that hands are used for nurturing.

Training in Right Behavior

Discipline is more than punishment for a wrong act; it's training in right behavior. The Hebrew word for *discipline* denotes "chastening, correction, rebuke, upbringing, training, instruction, education, and reproof." The word comes from the root word *disciple,* which means "one who is a follower of a teacher, a student."[1] Our children are students of life, learning how to follow Christ, relate to those around them, and become mature physically, emotionally, and spiritually as we disciple them in all these skills. When we instruct them, our challenge is to strive for balance between love and discipline.

Stanley Coopersmith, associate professor of psychology at the University of California, studied 1,738 middle-class boys and their families, beginning in the preadolescent period and following them to young manhood. He compared the homes of the boys who had high self-esteem with those of the boys who had low self-esteem, and he found three key distinguishing characteristics.

First, the high self-esteem boys came from homes where they felt deeply and genuinely loved and appreciated. Their self-worth was bolstered by the assurance of parental pride and interest in their activities.

Second, the boys with high self-esteem came from homes where their parents were considered stricter in their discipline. The boys from homes that demanded the strictest accountability and responsibility also had stronger family ties than the homes in which rules were lenient and unenforced. The boys in the lower self-esteem group interpreted their parents' permissiveness to mean no one cared enough to be involved.

And third, boys of the high self-esteem group experienced a home atmosphere of acceptance and emotional safety, which fostered freedom for them to express themselves without fear of ridicule and rejection. The boundaries were marked by their parents, but the sense of openness and democracy left room for discussion and personal growth.[2]

Note that the number one key to well-adjusted children was love, and right on love's coattails was discipline. We need to realize that if we don't discipline our child with love in his little world under our roof, he will be disciplined without love in the big world when he's on his own.

Diligent Discipline

Let's go back to Proverbs 13:24. The *New American Standard* version expresses it this way: "He who spares his rod hates his son, but he who loves him disciplines him *diligently*" (emphasis mine). In Hebrew, the word *diligently* means "to pursue something early on, or early in life."[3] Discipline begins the first time Junior puckers up his little lips, places his chubby hands on his hips, looks you defiantly in the eye, and forms the word *no.*

Zig Ziglar noted:

At no time is the mother more important in determining the direction in the child's life than during the early years. At no other time are the mother's own purpose, persuasion, personhood, and goals more significant. . . . The mother, because of her closeness, becomes the child's moral compass. Of course, the father is important during these years, especially as he stands strong beside his wife with love and warm emotional support to both mother and child.[4]

I especially remember my authority's being challenged when we had a ten-year-old foreign exchange student living with us for six weeks. When Andre came waltzing into my house, it quickly became apparent he was on vacation from all authority. My every request was met with his answering no. The requests were never unreasonable: "Andre, put on your coat." "Andre, it's time to go to bed." "Andre, it's time to take a bath."

The first time he said no, my son, who was also ten years old, just looked at me, then at Andre, and then back at me. Steven's look was not "What country are you from?" but "What planet are you from?" He was waiting to see what I would do. Well, I couldn't spank a child who wasn't my own, so I kept repeating the requests until one of us got tired. It was never I. My favorite line was, "In America, parents are the boss." (Of course, we all know that's not always true.)

I'll have to admit, when a little two-year-old forms the word *no* with cherub lips, it's kind of cute. But when a ten-year-old or a sixteen-year-old spits out the same word, it's no longer cute. The time to begin discipline is early. If we wait until a child is a teen, it may be too late.

It takes a diligent and determined mother to consistently discipline her child. After a long day of running errands, cooking, cleaning, washing clothes, ironing, and so on, it's much easier to turn a deaf ear to a sarcastic comment or a blind eye to Johnny who sneaks his hand into the forbidden cookie jar. I've let discipline slide on days when I've just been too tired to deal with another thing. But it seems I always ended up paying the price later. Discipline takes discipline, and it can make or break a child.

Susanna Wesley said:

> In order to firm the minds of children, the first thing to be done is to conquer their will and bring them to an obedient temper. To inform the understanding is a work of time, and must with children proceed by small degrees as they are able to hear it; but subjecting the will is a thing that must be done at once, and the sooner the better, for by neglecting timely correction they will contract a stubbornness and obstinacy which can hardly ever after be conquered, and never without using severity as would be as painful to me as to the children.[5]

Susanna was no pushover. Author Arnold Dallimore had this to say about her disciplinary strictness:

> It has been suggested that this principle would make children spineless automatons, yet the Wesley children grew up to be men and women who showed great strength of character, one of them to the degree superior to almost all others of his time. Susanna trained her children to obey and in so doing, she richly molded their characters.[6]

I see many haggard moms worn down by small acts of disobedience that occur over and over again. Many of these problems grew from small infractions that weren't corrected. If you see leniency starting to snowball in your home, call a family meeting. Apologize to your young children for not correcting them and giving them the discipline they so richly deserve. Assure them that, from now on, you will meet each act of disobedience with consistent, swift correction. Then stand back and wait for them to test your mettle!

Another verse on discipline states, "My son, do not reject the discipline of the Lord, or loathe His reproof, for whom the Lord loves He reproves, even as a father, the son in whom he delights" (Proverbs 3:11 NASB). The word *reproof* suggests "a good talking to."[7] If a child is punished, she needs to know why. Explain what she has done wrong and make sure she understands where she crossed the line.

As a child grows into adolescence, the paddle is put away, and verbal correction is the method of choice. The child is moving into adulthood, and spanking is reserved for children. Spanking a teenager can be humiliating and degrading to the child who is nearing adulthood. Actually, at times he might prefer a spanking to get it over with.

When my husband was in the ninth grade, he was caught wandering the halls and skipping shop class. When he was called into the principal's office, he was given two choices: three "licks" with a paddle or one strike on his record, which would mean he would be expelled from the National Honor Society. Steve chose the licks. When Steve told me about this incident, after I stopped laughing I asked him how it made him feel. He said with a smile, "It was very effective."

I'm not the authority on discipline. What works for one child won't necessarily work for another. That's when we go back to James 1:5, "If any of you lacks wisdom, he should ask God, who gives generously to all without finding fault, and it will be given to him."

Releasing the Angel

God uses trials and testing to discipline us, His children. We are His workmanship, and He constantly is chipping away at our rough edges to form us into Christ's image. For a short period of time, He places the mallet and chisel into a parent's hands to sculpt a child's heart.

I'm reminded of a story of the famous sculptor Michelangelo. One day a giant piece of marble was delivered to his studio. The artist walked around the slab several times, ran his hand across its smooth surface, and even placed his cheek against its cool exterior. Finally, he picked up a mallet and chisel and delivered mighty blows in every direction. Small chips and large pieces of stone flew around the room. His apprentice, watching in amazement, shouted, "What are you doing? You're ruining a perfectly good piece of marble." To that Michelangelo responded, "There's an angel in there, and I've got to get her out."[8]

So it is with our children. There's an angel in there, and we've got to get her or him out. God has placed a beautiful piece of marble in our hands, and He has given us the honor of shaping and molding it for a short period of time. Don't give up. Don't give in.

CHAPTER TWENTY-SIX

Give It All to Him

*O*nce a distraught father had an unruly son with multiple physical and emotional problems. Many people even said the boy was possessed by a demon. The dad had tried everything, but the boy continued to demonstrate antisocial behavior, throwing himself into fire and then into water. That sort of behavior, on top of frequent seizures, rolling on the ground, foaming at the mouth, and an inability to talk, made the dad desperate to find a solution. He even took the boy to some faith healers who were traveling through his hometown. But nothing seemed to work.

Finally, the dad realized that no human being could help his son, so he took him directly to God. The father heard that Jesus was visiting in his community, so the man boldly brought the boy to Him. With desperation in his voice the father pleaded, "If You can do anything, take pity on us and help us!"

And Jesus answered, "If You can! All things are possible to him who believes."

Immediately the boy's father cried out, "I do believe; help my unbelief."

With that profession, Jesus healed the man's son.

This story from Mark 9 stirs my heart. Can't you feel the father's pain? How desperate he must have felt every time the child threw himself into the water or into the fire. "Why, Son? Why do you do these things?" he must have asked. "I don't understand."

Imagine the humiliation of hearing whispers as the family walked down the streets. "That's the Jones family. Have you heard about their son? He's . . ." The stares, the snickers, the cruel comments. Don't you know that on many days this dad wanted just to give up? Instead, he offers us a beautiful picture of what all parents must do (the ultimate act in parenting): Hand our children over to the Lord.

Sometimes, as mothers, we find ourselves at the end of our mental and emotional resources. We feel we've done everything humanly possible and don't know what next action to take with our children. That's exactly where God wants us every day, not depending on our human capabilities but on His insurmountable omniscience, not depending on our own strength but on His unlimited power. When we realize we don't and never will have all the child-rearing answers, we discover the importance of giving our children to God.

S. D. Gordon in *Quiet Talks on Prayer* said, "You can do more than pray, after you have prayed. But you cannot do more than pray until you have prayed."[1]

Praying for Our Children

Earlier in this book, we talked about sowing seeds of prayer as we pray *with* our children. Now we turn our attention to praying *for* our children. A blessed mother realizes that, no matter what she does to develop her children's character, ultimately the choices are theirs to make. Just as we take our hands off the bicycle when the training wheels are removed, we eventually must release the child into the world. Then, when we no longer know what to do with hands that were once so busy, we fold them in prayer.

When our children are preschoolers, we tend to keep them close by our sides. We control everything they eat, see, smell, touch, and taste. Then one day they skip off to kindergarten. There, just as little Johnny and Susie are exposed to germs from putting hands, pencils, crayons, and other children's lunches in their mouths, so are they exposed to new "bad words" and other delightful horrors from children whose family values don't match our own. Protective moms of elementary-school-age children tend to remain pretty close, becoming room mothers, helping with class parties, and chaperoning field trips.

But the first thing I noticed when I walked the halls of middle school was the drastic reduction in the number of visible mothers. And the ones who were present had better have a good reason for being there—such as a death in the family.

Even though we aren't "allowed" to be as visible in an adolescent's life, that doesn't mean we can take a breather from parenting. Many times mothers say, "OK, I've trained him up, and he knows the rules. No more Valentine's parties. No more field trips. Now I can relax!" and off we go to do our own thing. Then—WHAM!—something happens to bring us back to reality and let us know that the job isn't finished yet.

Weeds Among the Wheat

This reminds me of the parable in Matthew 13:24–30. Jesus tells of a farmer who sowed good seed in his field, "but while everyone was sleeping, his enemy came and sowed weeds among the wheat, and went away." No one knew the enemy had even been to the field, because he came while they were sleeping. Then, when the wheat sprang up, the weeds became evident, also. The slaves who planted the wheat came to the landowner with the same question that many parents ask themselves when something goes wrong, "Sir, didn't you sow good seed in your field? Where then did the weeds come from?" A mother asks herself, "I've sown good seed: Bible memory, church, family devotions, youth group. How did this happen?" The answer for many of us is the same as it was for the workers in Matthew: "An enemy did this—while we were sleeping."

First Peter 5:8 says that our adversary "the devil prowls around like a roaring lion looking for someone to devour." And what better meat to devour than the tender lambs of youth? As he prowls around, may we never be caught off guard but stand firm in prayer.

Keep One Hat On

Mothers today wear many hats. Some we lay aside as our children grow to maturity. However, we should keep one hat in our wardrobe, the helmet of a faithful prayer warrior.

I've often heard people say, "You can't fight your children's battles for them." Well, I agree, and I disagree. It all depends on what battles they're referring to. A child on her way to adulthood should conquer some struggles herself. The butterfly must struggle to break free of the chrysalis. The chick must use his own strength to break free of the egg. It's part of the growth process, and, without it, neither winged creature can thrive. Likewise, overcoming obstacles makes us strong. For example, the eagle's only obstacle to flying with great ease and speed is the air. However, if the obstacle is removed (the air is withdrawn) and the eagle is placed in a vacuum, he couldn't fly at all. The very element that offers resistance to flying is the one that gives him the ability to soar. In that respect, a mother shouldn't always rush to rescue Junior when he runs into trouble.

However, one battle we can fight for our children—or at least by their side—is the spiritual one. Second Corinthians 10:3–4 says, "For though we walk in the flesh, we do not war according to the flesh, for the weapons of our warfare are not of the flesh, but divinely powerful for the destruction of fortresses"(NASB). Again, in Ephesians 6:10–12 we read, "Finally, be strong in the Lord, and in the strength of His might. Put on the full armor of God, that you may be able to stand firm against the schemes of the devil. For our struggle is not against flesh and blood, but against the rulers, against the powers, against the world forces of this darkness, against the spiritual forces of wickedness in the heavenly places" (NASB).

When Proverbs 31:10 introduces us to the mother whose children rise up and call her blessed, different translations have slightly different descriptions of her. The *New International Version* calls her "a wife of noble character"; the *New American Standard Bible* refers to her as "an excellent wife"; and my favorite, the *Amplified Bible,* describes her as "a capable, intelligent and virtuous woman." The actual Hebrew word for "excellent" or "virtuous" is *chayil,* which is sometimes translated "virtuous, boldly courageous, powerful, *mighty warrior.*"[2]

The mother whose children rise up and call her blessed is a warrior who battles in prayer for the hearts, minds, and souls of her children. She prays a hedge of protection around them and stands in the gap when they don't know how to pray for themselves. She meets the Enemy head-on, dressed in God's armor and with the sword of the Spirit (the Word of God) drawn and ready for action. We may never know the many times the Enemy's schemes against our children were thwarted by the power of our prayers.

Unburdened

You may feel at times that your burden for your child is more than you can bear. Peter tells us to "cast all our anxiety on him because he cares for you" (1 Peter 5:7). He cares for your children too. No matter how much you love your children, God loves them more.

I mentioned earlier being a camel mom, who stores up her good memories for the desert days. Another characteristic of a camel is that it bends its long legs and kneels before its master so the master can remove the burdens from its back. We need to have camel knees, knees that become wrinkled and callused from kneeling before the Lord as we ask Him to remove the burdens that are too heavy for us to carry. Especially in the final years of parenting, we have to practice having camel knees, letting go of our children and placing them in the capable hands of our heavenly Father.

But letting go isn't always easy.

> Just as my child brings his broken toys
> With tears for me to mend,
> I took my broken dreams to God
> Because He was my friend,
> But then . . . instead of leaving Him in peace to work alone,
> I hung around and tried to help
> With ways that were my own.
> At last I snatched them back and cried,
> "How could You be so slow?"
> "What could I do, My child?" He said.
> "You never did let go."
>
> —Faith Mitchner[3]

In my Bible I keep a four-by-six-inch laminated card with prayers for Steven that are my defense against the Enemy's attack. You too can pray that your children will

* Know Christ as Savior early in life (Psalm 63:1; 2 Timothy 3:15)
* Have a hatred for sin (Psalm 97:10)
* Be caught when guilty (Psalm 119:71)
* Be protected from the Evil One in each area of their lives: spiritual, emotional, and physical (John 17:15)
* Have a responsible attitude in all their interpersonal relationships (Daniel 6:3)
* Respect those in authority over them (Romans 13:1)
* Desire the right kind of friends and be protected from the wrong friends (Proverbs 1:10–11)
* Be kept from the wrong mate and saved for the right one (2 Corinthians 6:14–17)
* Be kept pure until marriage (as well as the one they marry) (1 Corinthians 6:18–20)
* Learn to submit totally to God and actively to resist Satan in all things (James 4:7)
* Be single-hearted, sold out to Jesus Christ (Romans 12:1–2)
* Be hedged in so they can't find their way to wrong people or wrong places and the wrong people can't find their way to them (Hosea 2:6)

CHAPTER TWENTY-SEVEN

Ruth Bell Graham:
A Diligent Mother

*R*uth McCue Bell was born June 10, 1920, the daughter of medical missionaries in mainland China. She spent the greater part of the '20s and '30s facing unspeakable hardship, surrounded by sickness and disease along with the tension of political unrest and military turmoil.

When she was seventeen, Ruth boarded a ship bound for the United States to further her education at Wheaton College in Illinois. While there, she met a fiery would-be evangelist from a dairy farm in Charlotte, North Carolina, who stole her heart. On August 13, 1943, Ruth Bell married this young man and became Mrs. Billy Graham.

The Grahams settled in Montreat, North Carolina, on 150 acres of heavily wooded mountain land, which they called Piney Cove. Mr. Graham spent many days on the road in response to God's call to preach the Gospel. Ruth kept the family intact. She was the bedrock of the Graham family, and, with five children at her heels, this was no easy task. Ruth understood that a blessed mother is one who is diligent, who doesn't give up, who doesn't give in, and who gives her children to God.

Of all the Graham children, perhaps the eldest son, William Franklin Graham III, was the one who required the most diligent mothering. On the day Franklin was born, the family received telegrams and cards that provided a glimpse into the pressure outsiders would place on him in the future. One Western Union telegram read, "Welcome to this sin-sick world and the challenge you have to walk in your daddy's footsteps." A card read, "May his great father's mantle fall on him." Another read, "Good luck and best wishes to the young preacher."[1]

Instead of following in his daddy's footsteps, however, young Franklin ran as fast as he could in the opposite direction. When Franklin was as young as three years old, he became fascinated with cigarettes. While building the Grahams' log home, construction workers threw their cigarette butts on the ground, and Franklin picked them up to smoke what was left. On several occasions, his mother caught him and gave stern lectures on the evils of smoking. But the habit continued to grow.

After several years, Ruth decided to teach Franklin a lesson. She borrowed a pack of cigarettes from the groundskeeper, sat Franklin down at the kitchen table, opened the pack, pulled out a cigarette, and handed it to him. "Now light it and smoke it—and be sure to inhale!" When he finished the first one, she handed him a second. Franklin threw up five or six times but stubbornly lit up cigarette after cigarette until the entire pack was gone. She had hoped this would make him sick enough to stop smoking, but it didn't work.

Franklin had little interest in spiritual things, even though he went to church every Sunday. Each morning after breakfast and each evening before bed, Ruth read to the children a Bible passage and prayed. She encouraged them to memorize Scripture. On Sundays after church, before the children could go out to play, they had to recite a Bible verse. Even though Franklin showed little responsiveness, she was diligent to sow the seeds.

He also had little interest in academics. When he was thirteen, his parents sent him to Stony Brook School for boys, an elite Christian boarding school on Long Island. This was Franklin's worst nightmare. The boy who loved blue jeans, cowboy boots, and camping in the woods was forced to wear a coat and tie to class every day. The highlight of his time there was receiving letters from his mother two to three times a week.

When she shared news, I could picture the log house and almost smell the chicken frying in Bea's pan. But more than anything else, Mama's letters were spiritually encouraging—like those penned by the apostle Paul writing the early church. Mama's letters always had a verse, a word of comfort from the Lord, a special lesson. She always concluded with her love and how proud she was of me. I treasured those letters and read them over and over.[2]

Franklin resented being at Stony Brook and became more and more rebellious, breaking the rules by smoking and drinking beer. Just before his senior year, he convinced his father to let him finish high school in Montreat, telling his dad that he probably was going to get kicked out if he didn't leave first. Back in North Carolina, his rebellious attitude continued. Only a few weeks after starting school there, he was suspended for fighting.

Many nights Ruth couldn't sleep, thinking about her son. So she turned to God in prayer. "Every time I pray especially for him, God says: 'Love him . . .' which seems odd because I love every bone of him. But God means show it. Let him in on the fact. Enjoy him. You think he's the greatest, let him know you think so."[3]

Another area in which Franklin rebelled was curfew. When he was out at night, Ruth always waited up for him. No matter how late it was when he returned, she didn't lecture but said something such as, "Thank God you're all right." After a while, he felt so ashamed about her losing sleep that he set his own curfew and started to come in on time. He knew that his mother was diligent. She wasn't going to change, so he had to—at least with the curfew.

One example of Ruth's diligence was her response when Franklin wouldn't be rousted out of bed in the morning. After growing tired of struggling to get him up, one day she dumped an ashtray full of cigarettes on his head. The next day, finding that he had locked his door, she slid a lit firecracker under his door. (That worked rather nicely.) The following day, Franklin put a towel under his locked door. When he heard her jingle the doorknob, he laughed to himself. But a few minutes later, he heard his brother's window open and looked out his window to see his mother crawling on all fours across the roof with a cup of water in her mouth. Quickly he locked his window and smiled like a Cheshire cat at her. She couldn't help but smile back.

Ruth reminds us that a diligent mom doesn't have to be a somber mom. "A merry heart doeth good like a medicine" (Proverbs 17:22 KJV)— to the child and to the mother who loves him.

Franklin went away to LeTourneau College in Texas but was expelled for breaking the rules during his first year. Back in Montreat, he attended Montreat Anderson College. Then he discovered racing dirt bikes, which he pursued with a passion on Sundays. Ruth was very upset and said, "Franklin, I'm praying that the Lord will do something to get your attention—break your leg or put you in the hospital. I have prayed, 'Lord, don't kill him, but do whatever it takes to get his attention.'"[4]

A few weeks later, he was riding his bike, caught the toe of his boot on a tree stump, and broke his foot. He decided to stop racing on Sundays.

But more than Franklin's stopping smoking, drinking, or racing, Ruth's heart's desire was for him to stop running from God and to give his life to Him. That was her prayer.

During the summer of 1974, Franklin could run no more. While reading John 3, he confessed to God that he was sick and tired of being sick and tired. He poured out his heart to God and confessed his sin. He told God he was sorry and that, if He would take the pieces of Franklin's life and somehow put them back together, he was God's. The running was over.

From that time on, he followed the Lord. Today, Franklin serves as president of Samaritan's Purse, a Christian relief and evangelism organization that spreads the Gospel by meeting the physical and spiritual needs of victims of war, famine, disease, and natural disasters.

Franklin Graham had rebelled during his youth, but he had a mother who never gave up on him. She said, "When folks say, 'You must be proud of Franklin,' we realize that it is not a matter of pride, but of gratitude to God for His faithfulness."[5]

THE WARRIOR

This morning my thought traveled along
To a place in my life where days have long since gone,
Beholding an image of what I used to be
As visions were stirred, and God spoke to me.

He showed me a Warrior, a soldier in place,
Positioned by Heaven, yet I saw not the face.
I watched as the Warrior fought enemies
That came from the darkness with distractions for me.

I saw as the Warrior would dry away tears
As all of Heaven's Angels hovered so near.
I saw many wounds on the Warrior's face.
Yet weapons of warfare were firmly in place.

I felt my heart weeping, my eyes held so much
As God let me feel the Warrior's prayer touch.
I thought "how familiar" the words that were prayed.
The prayers were like lightning that never would fade.

I said to God, "Please, the Warrior's name."
He gave no reply, He chose to refrain. I asked,
"Lord, who is broken that they need such prayer?"
He showed me an image of myself standing there.

Bound by confusion, lost and alone,
I felt prayers of the Warrior carry me home.
I asked, "Please show me, Lord, this Warrior so true."
I watched and I wept, for Mother . . .

The Warrior — was you!

—Larry Clark
Used by permission of the author

239

CHAPTER TWENTY-EIGHT

Just a Mom,
You Say?

"I'm just a mom,"
I overheard her say,
With eyes downcast
And a look of dismay.

I turned with a start
And enthusiastically decreed,
"A mom, did you say?
Oh, can it be?

"For a mom is a beacon
Shining so bright,
A landmark by day,
And a light by night.

"She guides and protects
On land and at sea.
Did you say a mom?
Oh, can it be?

"She listens to stories
Woes and concerns,
With her eyes and her heart,
She quickly discerns.

"Questions she asks,
To draw children out.
Building godly ones
Is what she's about.

"She gives the gift
Of encouraging words.
With courage and strength
Their souls she girds.

"She cheers them up,
When they are down,
And turns sad days,
Completely around.

"She says, 'You can do it!
I know that you can!'
And develops a boy
Into a man.

"She builds self-esteem
Into young hearts.
Jesus Christ's power,
She thus imparts.

"'Who am I?'
She hears them say.
'You are God's child,
Loved—come what may.'

"Foundations of love,
Walls capable and strong,
Valued, adored,
They know they belong.

"She sows seeds of Scripture,
Day after day,
And sows seeds of prayer,
That help point the way.

"She guards information
That goes in their heads
And whispers a prayer
As they're tucked into beds.

"She sets an example
Of how they should live,
Of how our Father
Can quickly forgive.

"Love, joy, and peace,
Is what they see,
Knowing the example she sets,
Is what they will be.

"She never gives up
When life gets tough.
And doesn't give in
When kids get rough.

"A warrior, a fighter,
She diligently prays,
And then at God's feet
Her children she lays.

"'Just a mom,' you say?
What an honor bestowed,
A beacon, a builder,
With many seeds sowed.

"A listener, encourager,
Diligent too.
A mom, how bless-ed.
My hat's off to you!"

I finished my sermon,
Not making a scene,
And transformed before me,
She looked like a queen.

Her eyes now beaming,
She sat tall and erect.
"Excuse me, sir,
I spoke incorrect.

"God gave me a job,
That compares to none other,
Esteemed and chosen by Him.
You see, I'm a mother."

—Sharon Jaynes

CHAPTER TWENTY-NINE

A Mother Counts Her Blessings

Every mother finds the growth and development of her child amazing. That's because it truly is. Here's a peek at the rewards we each experience as we work hard to be a mother whose children call her blessed. I wrote this piece to Steven the day I took him to get his driver's permit.

I crept into your room today as the sun was peeking over the horizon. A single ray of light reaches through the blinds and illuminates your angelic face like a lone actor on a stage. Two tiny fists frame your olive face as you snuggle peacefully under your yellow blanket.

A small head, capped with black, bushy hair. Long, Bambi-like eyelashes. Perfectly formed cherub lips. A red forceps mark on your forehead. Knees curled and tucked under your tummy.

A mound of love that just three days before kicked my ribs and moved inside my tummy now sleeps in a crib and moves my heart.

Yellow gingham bumper pads frame this picture of sweetness, tranquility, and love. I drink in the scent of baby powder, fresh wipes, and lotion. The room overflows with toys: a Noah's ark soft-sculpted toy with ten bulging pockets carrying animals two-by-two, a bunny-shaped rattle, a tinkling music box. Stuffed animals with bright satin bows huddle in a corner. A white wicker rocker beckons.

I stroke your head and watch you breathe, finding my chest in sync with yours. Three days old. My precious gift from God. What journeys await our family of three?

I crept into your room today and thanked God for the wonder of you.

* * *

I crept into your room today before my little man awoke. In just a few minutes you would be calling out in your two-year-old voice for Mommy and Daddy to get you out of your now-too-small crib for a little snuggle time before Dad goes off to work.

The black hair has been replaced with golden corn silk capping your precious head. Long, thick eyelashes, now dubbed "angel wings," rest on chubby cheeks. The yellow blanket that once kept you warm now keeps you secure as you clutch it tightly to your side. Somehow your thumb has found its way to your mouth, and I hear the sound of gentle sucking.

Big Bird and Ernie wait patiently for their little friend to stir. A train stands parked in the corner. A stick horse is tethered to the doorknob. Rubber balls and wooden blocks rest in a basket. Pop-up books, Richard Scarry, *Lowly Worm, Busy People, Things That Go*—all your familiar friends crowd on the bookshelf. Wooden puzzles, plastic trucks, cardboard tubes for jousting lie where you dropped them. The well-worn wicker rocker has become my favorite spot in the house.

I stroke your blond head and watch your gentle breathing, still amazed that so much love could be found in one small package.

I crept into your room today and thanked God for the wonder of you.

* * *

I crept into your room today, your first day of school. In Superman pajamas, hugging a well-worn teddy bear, you dreamed of new friends and adventure. A shiny new red lunch box sits on the dresser. Stiff new jeans and a crisply striped knit shirt await you. A blue backpack stuffed with fresh crayons, markers, and wide-ruled notebook paper hangs from the doorknob.

Plastic swords, a play mobile, plastic Indians, Nerf balls, a sheriff's badge, and cowboy boots all will remain motionless today. A T-ball trophy on the dresser and a team picture of twelve miniature athletes in a red frame on the wall trumpet your interest in sports.

I stroke your sandy blond head, and tears stream down my cheeks. In just a few minutes, I'll be walking you down the sidewalk and entrusting my most valued possession into the hands of another woman. Will your teacher know that you are the most creative child God ever fashioned? Will she discover you already know your ABCs and can count to 100? Will she know that you asked Jesus to come into your heart and can recite the Lord's Prayer and Twenty-third Psalm? Will she know that you need lots of hugs? Will she know that this is one of the hardest days of my life? Oh, how I'm going to miss my little man today.

I crept into your room today and thanked God for the wonder of you.

* * *

I crept into your room today before the sun made its way into the sky. You, my little soldier, lay tangled in the sheets with Beary the white polar bear tucked under your arm. He was staring admiringly into his charge's tranquil face.

The cars-and-trucks wallpaper has been replaced with a plaid coat-of-arms. Baseball hats hang from the corners of your four-poster bed. Soccer pictures line the walls. A Boy Scout handbook and well-worn matchbox cars parked in a slotted carrying case litter the floor. Stray Legos peek from under the bed. G. I. Joes, who are back from their latest mission, share a shelf with hard-to-part-with stuffed animals. A flashlight rests on *The Chronicles of Narnia*.

I stroke your head and wonder if you have any idea how much I've loved being your mom for these past ten years.

I crept into your room today and thanked God for the wonder of you.

* * *

I crept into your room today before the day was new. Breaking all the new rules of privacy and personal space, I gaze with awe at my twelve-year-old young man.

Michael Jordan grins at me from a poster taped on the closet door. Muddy baseball pants hang over a chair. Inverted tube socks are wadded up and tossed in a corner. A CD player, headphones, magazines, deodorant, boxers, and fuzzy legs all make me dizzy to think how quickly we've arrived at this point. Five-feet-nine-inches of muscle and bone, you are a man-child metamorphosing before my very eyes.

A school yearbook is opened to page 87 where a certain young lady's smiling face had been the last thing on your mind. A new era is on the horizon. I whisper a prayer over your sleeping form as I rub your sandy head. A prayer of protection, purity, and purpose.

I crept into your room today and thanked God for the wonder of you.

* * *

I crept into your room today before the alarm signaled the dawn of a new day. Your six-foot frame lies angled across the mattress. A man's hairy leg peeks out from under the tangled sheet. Your face needs a shave. A muscular arm hugs a willing pillow. Your chubby cheeks and pug nose have been replaced with handsome, angular lines. A strong jawbone. A determined nose. A thick shock of unruly hair.

A geometry book leans against the dresser. Ribbons and plaques from races won hang from the floor-lamp arm. A rack of neckties and khakis mingle with T-shirts and jeans. A track team warm-up suit is slung over a chair. A basketball letter and pin leans against the mirror. An electric guitar, amplifier, distorter, and Christian punk CDs shout out the new era we're in. A Tarheels license plate rests on an easel, pointing to future dreams.

My little boy has become a man, in the twinkling of an eye, in the flash of a moonbeam, in the time it takes a shooting star to traverse the night sky. I smooth your thick hair and watch your chest rise and fall. What a gift you've been to me. How will I ever let you go?

Today I drive you to the Department of Motor Vehicles to pick up your license to new freedoms. I go as a driver but return as a passenger. A tear escapes my eye and trickles down my chin as I'm reminded once again that this chapter of my life is coming closer to an end.

I crept into your room today and thanked God for the wonder of you.

Handwritten annotations (top left):

NLT
capable
enriching
(grocery shopper)
planner
planter
energetic
strong
hard worker
busy hands
helps needy
quilter
wise
virtuous

Handwritten annotations (top right):

MSG
· shops
· makes
· creates
· prepares
· organizes
· uses time + money wisely
· works hard
· skilled in the crafts of home
· diligent
· helpful
· designer
· satisfied
· content
· kind
· watches out for her family

Handwritten (center):

confidence in God despite difficult circumstances

A Look at God's Good Word To Mothers

*T*hese Bible studies provide you with a chance to look over what God has to say about this business of being a blessed mother. Each section in the book is covered in two lessons, with fourteen lessons in all. You can use them for personal contemplation or to gather together a group of other moms. Either way, you'll be bound to learn more about being a great mom, raising great kids.

Handwritten: her appearance is never mentioned

Section 1: Be a Beacon

Lesson 1: The Task of Watching

Handwritten: attractiveness comes from within

1. Read Proverbs 31:10–31 and list ways the wife of noble character took care of her family in King Lemuel's day. What would be parallel tasks for a modern mom? *Handwritten:* work hard, make wise financial decisions, use kind words

2. Look up in a dictionary and record the definition of "blessed" as used in verse 28.

Handwritten: held in reverence venerated; esteemed — bringing pleasure & contentment

3. Why do you think the phrase "rise up" (NASB) was used in verse 28 to describe her children's response?

NLT "stand" — *show respect*

4. Proverbs 31:27 says a wife of noble character "watches over the affairs of her household." What did the individuals in the verses listed below experience as they watched? How do those experiences correlate with a mother who watches? *for the betterment or protection of others*

longing
supportive
24-7
consistent
stand firm
always on

• Psalm 130:6
  long for the Lord (anticipation)

• Matthew 26:40–41
  they fell asleep — spirit willing, body weak

• Luke 2:8
  guarding flocks of sheep

• 1 Corinthians 16:13
  Be on guard, stand firm, be courageous, be strong

• 1 Peter 5:8
  Be careful — be alert — be perceptive

5. How is a mother's watchfulness like a beacon? *guiding light*
   You are putting a protective comfortable, safe place, covering over children

Lesson 2: This Little Light of Mine

In Bible times, homes were lit by oil lamps instead of candles. A major difference between the two is that a candle burns by consuming itself whereas an oil lamp burns by consuming fuel from an outside source poured into it. Keep this in mind as we learn more about oil.

1. How does Proverbs 31:18b make you feel as a mother?
   tired, exhausted, fatigued

2. Read Exodus 27:20–21. How long were the lamps in the tabernacle to be lit?
   continually

3. What does Jesus call Himself in John 8:12?
   Light of the World

4. In Matthew 5:14, what does Jesus call those who believe in Him?
   Light of the World

5. What source of fuel does Christ promise us in Acts 1:8?
   Holy Spirit

6. We are commanded to take what action step regarding the Holy Spirit in Ephesians 5:18? If we think of ourselves as a lamp needing the fuel of the Holy Spirit, what would the phrase "be filled" mean?

Don't be drunk u/ wine

be completely saturated, be controlled, be fueled, be powered by

7. What adjustments can you make in your life that will enable you to be a beacon, illumining your home with the glow of Christ?

Consistent quiet time, deeper prayer life

8. Circle which is true of you:

> • I'm burning my light as a candle that consumes itself.
>
> > *BOTH*
>
> • I'm burning like an oil lamp fueled by the Holy Spirit's oil.

9. Write a prayer asking God to fuel you with the power of His Spirit.

Section 2: Be a Listener

Lesson 3: I'm All Ears

1. What do the following verses teach us about listening to the Lord?

   • Proverbs 8:34 *Happy are those who listen to me*

   • John 18:37 *?*

   • Hebrews 3:7–8 *you must listen to His voice, don't harden your heart*

   • James 1:19 *be quick to listen*

2. In chapter 3, I mentioned that oil depleters could keep us from hearing the still small voice of God. Make a list of the oil depleters in your life. *(Telephone, computer, TV) no rest, over-committing, too much going on*

3. In the above list, which, if any, of the depleters can be eliminated? Which ones might not be God's call for you at this time? *Gems, CareNet, School Committee, Awana*

4. In Exodus 3:1–3, Moses "turn[ed] aside," as the *New American Standard Bible* expresses it. As a busy mother, what specific steps can you

Say aloud NO to the devil & a quiet yes to God

take to "turn aside" to listen to God's gentle whisper? To "turn aside"
to hear what your children are trying to tell you?
make eye contact, stop what I am doing

5. How, as Psalm 119:105 says, does God illuminate our path through His
   Word? it is a lamp unto my feet and a light unto my path

6. What can we hope to "hear" from God as we pray, according to

   • James 1:5 God will tell you what to do

   • Psalm 32:8 He will guide me, He will advise me, He will watch me

7. Set a time each day to be alone with God, reading His Word and listening in prayer. You could read one chapter of Proverbs each day. Since
   Proverbs contains 31 chapters, you would read the whole book in one
   month. Or, if you're fairly new to your relationship with God, you could
   begin by reading the gospel of John.

Lesson 4: Hearing Aids
1. How, in light of Proverbs 20:5, can a mother draw out the inner
   thoughts and desires of her child?
   understanding draws them out.

2. In the following verses, what function did Jesus hope His questions
   would serve for His listeners? Put a check mark by the verses contain-
   ing questions that you believe God would like to pose to you.

   • Matthew 5:13 how can it be made salty again?

   ✓ • Matthew 5:46 if you ♡ those who ♡ you — what reward is it?

   ✓ Matthew 9:28 Do you believe that I am able to do this?

   • Matthew 16:13-15 who do you say I am?

   • John 8:10 Woman, where are they? Has no one condemned you?

• John 18:34 *Is that your own idea?*

3. What did Jesus do during mealtime to stimulate conversation? How can you use those techniques to stimulate mealtime conversation at your house? *He told stories to illustrate the main point*

   • Luke 7:36–47

   • Luke 10:38–42 *resolved conflict peacefully by pointing out 'the better' choice*

   • John 21:15–17 *by asking questions w/ their repetition*

4. What perspectives about children can we learn from Jesus' treatment of them (Matthew 19:13–15)? *He welcomed them*

5. Think of a time when you were speaking and the person to whom you were talking appeared not to be listening. How did that person communicate that he or she wasn't listening? Are you guilty of those same non-listening habits with your children? If so, what can you do to change them?

6. If you are in a group, act out the following role play. Ask one person to tell about her most recent visit to the grocery store. While she is speaking, have the others in the group avoid eye contact with her, flip through papers, rummage through their pocketbooks, or whisper to their neighbors. Discuss how it felt not to be listened to and how it felt not to listen.

Section 3: Be an Encourager *according to their needs*

Lesson 5: Kind Words

be specific

1. In Ephesians 4:29, what do you think the phrase "unwholesome talk" means? *foul or abusive language (spirit crushing)*

2. List five examples of words that would build up someone, as verse 29 suggests. *good, helpful words. I believe in you, you have what it takes, you're special to me, I like your gentle spirit…*

3. What, according to that verse, are we giving to the hearer? *encouragement*

[Handwritten left margin: God's Riches At Christ's Expense]

[Handwritten above header: undeserving, unmerited favor]

4. The King James and *New American Standard* versions both say that we are giving or ministering "grace" to the hearer. How can our words give grace? *[handwritten: our words give grace by helping + healing - peacefully]*

5. Rewrite Ephesians 4:29 in your own words, based on your understanding of the key words. Add the phrase "my children" at the end of the verse.

6. Read the words Paul uses to encourage the church in Ephesians 1:15–21; 3:14–19; and Philippians 1:3–11. Pick one of those passages to use as a model to write a letter to your child. You might want to begin the letter with "I pray, [child's name] . . ."

[handwritten: spiritual wisdom, empowering, thanksgiving]

[handwritten: † all 3 †]

7. As a child, what were the most encouraging words anyone ever spoke to you? As an adult? Why do you think we're able to remember such moments? *[handwritten: You're good w/ kids. You're a good leader/writer]*

[handwritten left margin: talk slow soft]

Lesson 6: Silver Boxes

1. List the positive and negative repercussions of how we use our tongues, according to the verses below.

[handwritten left margin: impetuous, blurting out, not thinking first, talebearer, rashly]

- Proverbs 10:13 *[handwritten: wise words = discerning, understanding; fools are punished, hurt]*

- Proverbs 10:19 *[handwritten: Don't talk too much. Be sensible, nagging]*

- Proverbs 10:20 *[handwritten: godly words = sterling, key; fools are worthless (soft spoken) (gentle)]*

- Proverbs 10:21 *[handwritten: godly give good advice]*

- Proverbs 10:31 *[handwritten: godly = wise]*

- Proverbs 10:32 *[handwritten: perverted deceitful = cut off]*

- Proverbs 11:13 *[handwritten: gossip spreads secrets, wise keeps a confidence]*

- Proverbs 12:18 *[handwritten: godly speak what is helpful, wicked speak what is corrupt, rashly words of the wise bring healing]*

- Proverbs 13:3 *Control tongue = long life quick retort = ruin everything*
- Proverbs 15:1 *a gentle answer turns away wrath*
- Proverbs 16:21 *Kind words can calm wise = understanding & appreciate*
- Proverbs 16:24 *Kind words = like honey, sweet & healthy*
- Proverbs 25:11 *Timely advice is as lovely as golden apples in a silver basket*
- Proverbs 25:20 *Singing cheerfully to a sad person hurts them*
- Proverbs 31:26 *speaks with wisdom & kindness*

2. According to Matthew 15:18, where should we begin the work of taming the tongue? *heart*

3. Write out Psalm 19:14 as a prayer for the words you speak and think. *words & thoughts be pleasing*

4. When were you discouraged "by a sharp and cruel word," as the poem "Silver Boxes" expresses it?

5. What "silver box" can you bestow on your child today? Make specific plans to do so.

Section 4: Be a Self-Esteem Builder

Lesson 7: Building Your House *love your husband*

1. Read Proverbs 14:1. What are some ways a woman builds her house? What are some ways she tears it down? *encouragement / criticism*

2. What role does a mother's self-esteem play in the building up or tearing down of her house?

3. Where did David's confidence to fight Goliath come from, according to 1 Samuel 17:37? *the Lord*

4. Where does Psalm 127:1 tell us we should get our confidence to be great mothers? *The Lord*

5. Moses wasn't feeling too good about himself when God called him to lead the Israelites out of Egypt. How did God encourage him (Exodus 3:12, 17, 20; and 4:12)? *I will be with you*

6. How can we apply the promises God made to Moses to our insecurities about mothering? *Know that God is in control*

7. Review the list "Who Am I?" (pp. 133-34), choose three verses, and memorize them with your child this week.

Lesson 8: Such a Great Love

1. How do the verses listed below make you feel about yourself? About your relationship to God? What do all these verses have in common?

   - 1 John 3:1 *heavenly Father loves me. I am a child*

   - 1 John 4:9–10 *He loves me & sent His Son for me*

   - 1 John 4:16b *I know how much God loves me, and I put my trust in him.*

   - John 3:16

   - Romans 5:8 *my sin is no longer counted against me.*

   - Ephesians 2:4 *He loves me so very much*

   - Ephesians 3:19 *His love is so great I'll never understand it*

   - Jeremiah 31:3 *everlasting, unfailing love*

2. According to 1 John 4:19, why do we love God? If that's true, why will our children love us? *He first loved us*

3. Why does love build our self-esteem? *It fills us up with goodness*

4. How can you love your child more unconditionally? Write a prayer, asking God to help you know how to love your child in such a way that he or she will be able to receive that love.

Section 5: Be a Seed Sower

Lesson 9: Scripture Is . . .

1. How can Scripture be used in parenting, according to 2 Timothy 3:16?

2. When Jesus was confronted by Satan in Matthew 4:1–11, to what resource did He always turn to fend off Satan? In what ways would you need to prepare to be able to use Scripture in the same manner?

3. What directives does Deuteronomy 6:6–9 give us regarding Scripture?

4. What specific steps can you take to institute those verses in Deuteronomy into your home life?

5. What fruit will Scripture bear in your family's life?

   • Romans 10:17

   • Colossians 3:16

Lesson 10: Weeding and Sowing

1. Who were the seed sowers in Timothy's life according to 2 Timothy 1:5?

2. Exodus 2:1–10 and 1 Samuel 1:21–24 tell us about two other mothers. How long did each of them have to sow seeds in their sons' lives? (Hebrew children usually were weaned at two to three years of age.)

3. If you knew you had only three years to influence your child to follow God, how would you spend that time?

4. What are some of the weeds mentioned in Galatians 5:19–21 and Ephesians 4:25–26; 5:3–5 that we might need to pull out of our children's (and our own) lives?

5. What thoughts and images does Philippians 4:8 tell us we should sow in our children?

6. Create two columns, making a list at the left of weeds to pull in your child's life and a list at the right of seeds to sow.

Section 6: Be an Example Setter

Lesson 11: "Follow My Example, Children"

1. What would keep you from saying to your children, as Paul did in Philippians 3:17, "Follow my example"?

2. What kind of example did Jesus set for His disciples as described in John 13:12–17 and Philippians 2:5–11?

3. In 1 Timothy 4:12, what did Paul suggest Timothy do to be an example?

4. In 1 Peter 5:1–3, what attitudes were the church leaders encouraged to adopt?

5. What adjustments does this study suggest to you to make in the example you set for your children?

6. Hebrews 11 records the example of heroes of the faith. Use this chapter as a springboard to read stories of Bible heroes to your children. (Your concordance can help you find the story for each hero.)

Lesson 12: Tricksters

1. Rebekah started a cycle of trickery in her family when she set a bad example (Genesis 27). List the ways she used deception.

2. How did Jacob follow Rebekah's bad example (Genesis 27:18–27)?

3. We've all heard the saying "What goes around, comes around." What happened to Jacob after he had worked seven years for the hand of Rachel (Genesis 29:15–30)?

4. How did Jacob in turn deceive his father-in-law (Genesis 30:25–43)?

5. Later, Jacob had twelve sons who continued the cycle of trickery (Genesis 37:14–28). What did they do?

6. As a mother, what cycles did you "inherit" from your family? What can you do to break them so that you don't pass them on to your children?

Section 7: Be Diligent

Lesson 13: The Child Who Messed Up

1. King David, considered one of the heroes of the faith, was chosen by God while still in his teens, based on what criterion according to 1 Samuel 16:1–13?

2. What are two examples of David's success found in 1 Samuel 17:1–11, 41–50; and 1 Samuel 23:1–5?

3. To whom did David turn when he needed to make the decision recorded in 1 Samuel 23:2, 4,10,11?

4. What blunders did David make (2 Samuel 11)?

5. What happened as a result of David's sins recorded in 2 Samuel 12:15–18?

6. Despite David's falling several more times, how does God describe him in Acts 13:22?

7. How do you think God came to this conclusion?

8. As you consider the ways your child has failed and disappointed you, how can you come to the conclusion God did about David?

9. If you're having difficulty letting go of some way in which your child has disappointed you, write a prayer in which you express your feelings. Ask God to give you the ability to see your child through loving eyes and to let go of past failures. Ask for the ability to see your child as growing up to be a man or woman after God's own heart.

10. Commit to pray daily for your child's heart to become dependent on, fired up for, and sold out to Jesus Christ.

Lesson 14: Let's Close in Prayer

As we bring this study to a close, I want to encourage you to use Scripture to pray for your child. When mothers pray the Word of God, they pray the will of God. For example, Psalm 86:11–12 could be used to pray: "Teach Steven your way, O Lord, so that he will walk in your truth; give him an undivided heart, that he may fear your name."

No one can be a perfect parent, but everyone can be a praying parent. Read the following verses, inserting your child's name.

1. Romans 12:2

2. 1 Corinthians 6:19–20

3. 2 Corinthians 10:3–5

4. Ephesians 6:10–18

5. 1 Peter 2:9

6. 2 Timothy 2:2

7. 2 Timothy 2:15

8. 1 Peter 3:8

I wish I could be with each of you as you come to the close of this book. What an awesome job we have to raise great kids who love the Lord. Your giving a portion of your time to learn how to be a great mom tells me that you already are one. And for that, I rise up and call you blessed!

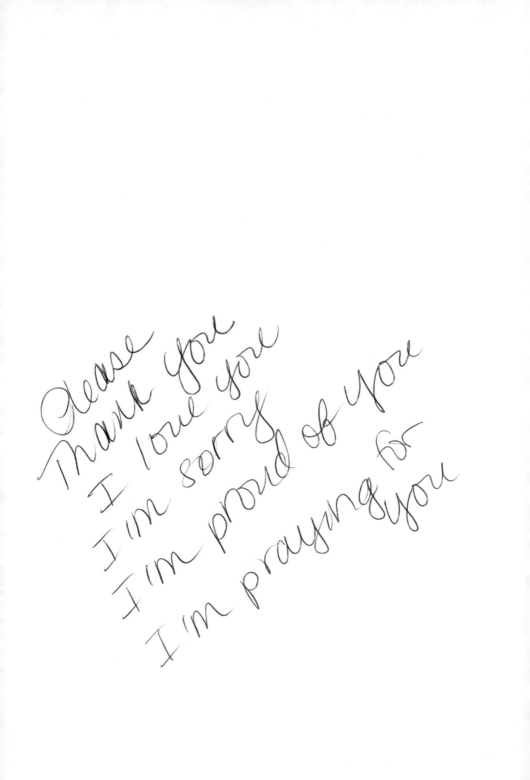

Notes

Chapter 1

1. Jack Canfield, Mark Victor Hansen, Jennifer Read Hawthorne, and Marci Shimoff, comps., *Chicken Soup for a Woman's Soul* (Deerfield Beach, Fla.: Health Communications, 1996), 163.

Chapter 2

1. Zig Ziglar, *Raising Positive Kids in a Negative World* (New York: Ballantine, 1989), 134.

2. Linda Webber, *Mom, You're Incredible* (Colorado Springs: Focus on the Family, 1994), 101.

3. Ziglar, 119.

4. Martha Miller, "Six Secrets to Raising Successful Teens," *Better Homes and Gardens,* October 1998, 112–23.

5. Brenda Hunter, *Home by Choice* (Sisters, Oreg.: Multnomah, 1991), 52.

6. William E. Vine, *Vine's Expository Dictionary of Old and New Testament Words* (Nashville: Nelson, 1985), 282.

7. Alice Gray, ed., *Stories for the Heart* (Sisters, Oreg.: Multnomah, 1996), 179.

Chapter 3

1. Charles Caldwell Ryrie, *Ryrie Study Bible* (Chicago: Moody, 1977), 1786.

2. *Just Like Jesus,* Max Lucado, Word Publishing, Nashville, Tennessee, 1998. All rights reserved, p. 97.

3. Jean Fleming, *A Mother's Heart* (Colorado Springs, Colo.: NavPress, 1982), 65.

4. Elizabeth George, *A Woman After God's Own Heart* (Eugene, Oreg.: Harvest House, 1997), 26.

5. Jack Canfield, Mark Victor Hansen, Jennifer Read Hawthorne, and Marci Shimoff, comps., *Chicken Soup for a Woman's Soul* (Deerfield Beach, Fla.: Health Communications, 1996), 178–80.

6. J. David Branon, "Sharing the Load," *Our Daily Bread,* June 1992, no. 3.

7. Armand M. Nicholi II, "The Fractured Family: Following It into the Future," *Christianity Today,* 25 May 1979, 12.

8. Robert D. Foster, *The Navigator* (Colorado Springs: NavPress, 1983), 110–11.

Chapter 4

1. Augustine, *Confessions* (New York: Penguin, 1961), 112.

2. Lindsey O'Connor, *Moms Who Changed the World* (Eugene, Oreg.: Harvest House, 1999), 57.

3. Joyce and H. Norman Wright, *Quiet Moments for Mothers* (Eugene, Oreg.: Harvest House, 1998).

Chapter 5

1. Kay Willis and Maryann Buckmum Brinley, "Sixteen Ways to Listen to Your Child," *Good Housekeeping,* August 1998, 158.

2. Dandi Daley Mackall, *Kids Are Still Saying the Darnedest Things* (Rocklin, Calif.: Prime Publishing, 1994), xii.

3. Ross Campbell, *How to Really Love Your Child* (Wheaton, Ill.: Victor, 1983), 18.

4. Mark Price, "Get a Life," *The Charlotte Observer,* 1 November 1998.

5. Dennis Rainey, *Staying Close* (Dallas: Word, 1989), 216.

6. Charles Swindoll, *The Grace Awakening* (Dallas: Word, 1990), 5–6.

7. Robert C. Crosby, *Now We're Talking! Questions That Bring You Closer to Your Kids* (Colorado Springs: Focus on the Family, 1996), xii.

8. Ibid., xiii.

9. Charles Caldwell Ryrie, *Ryrie Study Bible* (Chicago: Moody, 1977), 1778.

Chapter 6

1. David Jeremiah, *How to Encourage Your Children* (San Diego, Calif.: Turning Point for God, 1999), 8–9.

Chapter 7

1. Lindsay O'Connor, *Moms Who Changed the World* (Eugene, Oreg.: Harvest House, 1999), 13.

2. Nancee Skipper, "Mother's Day Confession," in *The Best of The Proverbs 31 Ministry* (Charlotte, N.C.: The Proverbs 31 Ministry, 1999), 227.

Chapter 8

1. William Barclay, The Letter to the Hebrews, *The Daily Study Bible* (Edinburgh: St. Andrews Press, 1955), 137–38.

2. Florence Littauer, *Silver Boxes* (Dallas: Word, 1989), 1–4.

3. Neil Anderson, *Victory over the Darkness* (Ventura, Calif.: Regal, 1990), 63.

4. "Mama's Plan," by Marion Bond West. Reprinted with permission from *Guideposts* magazine, (September 1988) copyright © 1988 by Guideposts, Carmel, New York 10512.

Chapter 9

1. Florence Littauer, *Silver Boxes* (Dallas: Word, 1989). Used by permission.

2. Ibid., 74.

3. Lysa Terkeurst, in *The Best of The Proverbs 31 Ministry* (Charlotte, N.C.: The Proverbs 31 Ministry, 1999), 214.

4. Zig Ziglar, *Raising Positive Kids in a Negative World* (New York: Ballantine, 1989), 54.

5. Charles Swindoll, *The Tale of the Tardy Oxcart* (Nashville: Word, 1998), 1.

6. Alan Loy McGinnis, *Bringing Out the Best in People* (Minneapolis: Augsburg, 1985), 118.

Chapter 10

1. Alan Loy McGinnis, *Bringing Out the Best in People* (Minneapolis: Augsburg, 1985), 75.

2. Author and original source unknown. Taken from *Victory over the Darkness* by Neil Anderson © 1990 Regal Books, Ventura, CA 93003. p. 114.

3. Jack Canfield and Mark Hansen, eds., *Chicken Soup for the Soul* (Deerfield Beach, Fla.: Health Communications, 1993), 228–30.

Chapter 11

1. Elizabeth Elliot, *A Chance to Die: The Life and Legacy of Amy Carmichael* (Grand Rapids: Revell, 1987), 26.

2. Kathleen White, *Amy Carmichael* (Minneapolis: Bethany House, 1986), 12.

3. Elliot, 55.

4. Lindsey O'Connor, *Moms Who Changed the World* (Eugene, Oreg.: Harvest House, 1999), 147.

5. Elizabeth George, *A Woman After God's Own Heart* (Eugene, Oreg.: Harvest House, 1997), 119.

Chapter 12

1. Tony Campolo, in *Stories for the Heart,* ed. Alice Gray, (Sisters, Oreg., Multnomah, 1996), 62.

2. Dorothy Corkill Biggs, *Your Child's Self-Esteem* (Garden City, N.Y.: Dolphin Books, 1975), 23.

Chapter 13

1. Ross Campbell, *How to Really Love Your Child* (Wheaton, Ill.: Victor, 1977), 30–31.

2. James Dobson, *Hide or Seek* (Old Tappan, N.J.: Revell, 1974), 23.

3. Eric Butterworth, "Love: The One Creative Source," in *Chicken Soup for the Soul* (Deerfield Beach, Fla.: Health Communications, 1993), 4.

4. William E. Vine, *Vine's Expository Dictionary of Old and New Testament Words* (Nashville: Nelson, 1985), 381–82.

Chapter 14

1. Source unknown, *Chicken Soup for the Soul,* ed. Jack Canfield and Mark Hansen (Deerfield Beach, Fla.: Health Communications, 1993), 74.

2. Linda Webber, *Mom, You're Incredible* (Colorado Springs: Focus on the Family, 1994), 33.

3. Nancy Aguilar, in *The Best of The Proverbs 31 Ministry* (Charlotte, N.C.: The Proverbs 31 Ministry, 1999), 104.

4. William Barclay, "Letters to the Galatians and Ephesians," *The Daily Study Bible* (Edinburgh: St. Andrews Press, 1962), 211.

5. Alan Loy McGinnis, *Bringing Out the Best in People* (Minneapolis: Augsburg,1985), 32.

6. Ibid., 32–33.

7. Ibid., 35.

8. P. D. Eastman, *Are You My Mother?* (New York: Random House, 1988).

Chapter 15

1. Zig Ziglar, *Raising Positive Kids in a Negative World* (New York: Ballantine, 1989), 179.

2. Ross Campbell, *How to Really Love Your Child* (Wheaton, Ill.: Victor, 1983), 41.

3. *Junior High Ministry,* May–August 1988, quoted in *The Josh McDowell Research and Statistics Digest,* 104.

4. Miles McPherson, *The Power of Believing in Your Child* (Minneapolis: Bethany House, 1998), 133–34.

5. Max Lucado, *You Are Special* (Wheaton, Ill.: Crossway, 1997).

Chapter 16

1. Source unknown, *Chicken Soup for the Soul,* ed. Jack Canfield and Mark Hansen, (Deerfield Beach, Fla.: Health Communications, 1993), 237.

2. Louis M. Notkin, ed., *Mother Tributes from the World's Great Literature* (New York: Samuel Curl, 1943), 117.

3. Joyce and H. Norman Wright, *Quiet Moments for Mothers* (Eugene, Oreg.: Harvest House, 1998).

4. Charles Swindoll, *Growing Wise in Family Life* (Portland, Oreg.: Multnomah, 1988), 69.

Chapter 17

1. Linda Webber, *Mom, You're Incredible* (Colorado Springs: Focus on the Family, 1994), 58.

2. Jean Fleming, *A Mother's Heart* (Colorado Springs: NavPress, 1982), 56.

Chapter 18

1. Elizabeth George, *A Woman After God's Own Heart* (Eugene, Oreg.: Harvest House, 1997), 105.

2. "Bible ABC's," created by Grace Wolgemuth (1976). Used with permission.

3. Carole C. Carlson, *Corrie Ten Boom: Her Life, Her Faith* (Old Tappan, N.J.: Revell, 1983), 33.

4. Stanley High, *Billy Graham* (New York: McGraw Hill, 1956), 126.

5. Charles R. Swindoll, *The Tale of the Tardy Ox Cart* (Nashville: Word, 1998), 202.

6. John Blanchard, comp., *Gathered Gold* (Durham, England: Evangelical Press, 1984), 14.

7. Sharon Jaynes, *At Home with God: Stories of Life, Love and Laughter* (Tulsa, Okla.: Honor Books, 2001).

Chapter 19

1. Dick Gilling and Robin Brightwell, *The Human Brain* (London: Orbis, 1982), 13.

2. "Sex and Violence in Media," North Carolina Family Policy Council, 6 January 1999.

3. Zig Ziglar, *Raising Positive Kids in a Negative World* (New York: Ballantine, 1989), 17.

4. Judith Newman, "Sex and the Prom," *Seventeen*, May 1991, 18.

5. Joe White, *Faith Trainers* (Colorado Springs: Focus on the Family, 1994), 47.

6. Miles McPherson, *The Power of Believing in Your Child* (Minneapolis: Bethany, 1998), 152.

7. Ibid., 153.

8. "Television Statistics," North Carolina Family Policy Council, 2 September 1999.

9. Rebecca A. Maynard, ed., *Kids Having Kids* (Robin Hood Foundation, 1996).

10. Ibid.

11. "Television Statistics."

12. "Television Statistics."

13. "Television Statistics."

14. "Sex and America's Teenagers" (New York: The Alan Guttmacher Institute, 1994), 31.

15. George J. Stevenson, *Memorials of the Wesley Family* (N.p.: Partridge, 1876), 164.

Chapter 20

1. Cecil Murphey and Nathan Aaseng, *Ben Carson* (Grand Rapids: Zondervan, 1992), 16.

2. Ibid., 22.

3. Ibid., 49.

4. Zig Ziglar, *Raising Positive Kids in a Negative World* (New York: Ballantine, 1989), 9.

Chapter 21

1. *The Best of The Proverbs 31 Ministry* (Charlotte, N.C.: The Proverbs 31 Ministry, 1999), 211–12.

2. Denise Foley and Eileen Nechas, "The Bodsquad," *Charlotte Observer,* 31 January 2000.

3. Glen Van Ekeren, *The Speaker's Source Book II* (Paramus, N.J.: Prentice Hall, 1994), 133.

4. Alice Gray, ed., *Stories for the Heart* (Sisters, Oreg.: Multnomah, 1996), 171.

5. Zig Ziglar, *Raising Positive Kids in a Negative World* (New York: Ballantine, 1989), 46.

6. Ann Ortlund, *Children Are Wet Cement* (Old Tappan, N.J.: Revell, 1981), 58.

7. Charles R. Swindoll, *Family Life* (Portland, Oreg.: Multnomah, 1988), 72.

8. Robert S. McGee, Jim Craddock, and Pat Springle, *The Parent Factor* (Houston: Rapha, 1989), 9.

9. Corrie ten Boom, *Tramp for the Lord* (Grand Rapids: Revell, 1974), 83.

10. Ibid., 82–86.

11. Glen Van Ekeren, *The Speaker's Source Book II* (Paramus, N.J.: Prentice-Hall, 1994), 325.

12. Ibid., 225.

13. Ziglar, 156.

14. Joe White, *Faith Trainers* (Colorado Springs: Focus on the Family, 1994), 38.

Chapter 22

1. John Blanchard, comp. *Gathered Gold* (Durham, England: Evangelical Press, 1984), 189.

2. Sharon Jaynes, *At Home with God: Stories of Life, Love and Laughter,* (Tulsa, Okla.: Honor Books, 2001).

3. William E. Vine, *Vine's Expository Dictionary of Old and New Testament Words* (Nashville: Nelson, 1985), 274.

4. Ron Green, "Ripken Earns Our Applause," *Charlotte Observer,* 7 September 1995.

5. Jan Karon, *At Home in Mitford* (Elgin, Ill.: Lion, 1994), 314.

6. Vine, 401.

Chapter 23

1. Joe White, *Faith Trainers* (Colorado Springs: Focus on the Family, 1994), 37–38.

Chapter 24

1. Zig Ziglar, *Raising Positive Kids in a Negative World* (New York: Ballantine, 1982), 311.

2. Lindsey O'Connor, *Moms Who Changed the World* (Eugene, Oreg.: Harvest House, 1999). 22.

3. Cited in *The Best of Bits and Pieces*.

4. Rob Gilbert, ed., *Bits and Pieces,* vol. N/4, 1.

5. Ziglar, 121.

6. Dorothy Patterson, "The High Calling of Wife and Mother in Biblical Perspective," in *Recovering Biblical Manhood and Womanhood,* ed. John Piper and Wayne Grudem. (Wheaton, Ill.: Crossway, 1991), 371.

7. Alice Gray, ed., *Stories from the Heart* (Sisters, Oreg.: Multnomah, 1996), 41.

Chapter 25

1. James Strong, *Strong's Exhaustive Concordance* (Grand Rapids: Baker, 1987), 4148.

2. James Dobson, *Hide or Seek* (Old Tappan, N.J.: Revell, 1979), 92–93.

3. Charles Swindoll, *Growing Wise in Family Life* (Portland, Oreg.: Multnomah, 1988), 118.

4. Zig Ziglar, *Raising Positive Kids in a Negative World* (New York: Ballantine, 1982), 79.

5. Arnold A. Dallimore, *Susanna Wesley: The Mother of John and Charles Wesley* (Grand Rapids: Baker, 1993), 11.

6. Ibid., 61.

7. Swindoll, 121.

8. Elizabeth George, *Loving God with All Your Mind* (Eugene, Oreg.: Harvest House, 1994), 160–66.

Chapter 26

1. Jean Fleming, *A Mother's Heart* (Colorado Springs: NavPress, 1982), 133.

2. Elizabeth George, *Beautiful in God's Eyes* (Eugene, Oreg.: Harvest House, 1998), 15.

3. Anabel Gillham, *The Confident Woman* (Eugene, Oreg.: Harvest House, 1993), 13.

Chapter 27

1. Franklin Graham, *Rebel with a Cause* (Nashville: Nelson, 1995), 1.

2. Ibid., 36.

3. Patricia Cornwell, *Ruth–A Portrait, the Story of Ruth Bell Graham* (New York: Doubleday, 1997), 186.

4. Graham, 109.

5. Ibid., 314.

About the Author

Sharon Jaynes , author of *The Ultimate Makeover, Celebrating a Christ-Centered Christmas,* and co-author of *Seven Life Principles for Every Women,* is the vice-president of **Proverbs 31 Ministries.** She is also co-host of the organization's international radio program and popular speaker for women's events from coast-to-coast. She and her husband, Steve and their son, Steven live in Charlotte, NC. For information on having Sharon Jaynes speak to your women's group, call or write **Proverbs 31 Ministries.**

About Proverbs 31 Ministry

Proverbs 31 Ministries is a non-denominational organization dedicated to glorifying God by touching women's hearts to build godly homes. Through Jesus Christ, we shed light on God's distinctive design for women and the great responsibilities we have been given. With Proverbs 31:10–31 as a guide, we encourage and equip women to practice living out their faith as wives, mothers, friends and neighbors.

What began in 1992 as a monthly newsletter has now grown into a multi-faceted ministry reaching women across the country and around the globe. Each aspect of the ministry seeks to equip women in the Seven Principles of **The Proverbs 31 Woman**.

1. The Proverbs 31 woman reveres Jesus Christ as Lord of her life and pursues an ongoing, personal relationship with Him.
2. The Proverbs 31 woman loves, honors, and respects her husband as the leader of the home.
3. The Proverbs 31 woman nurtures her children and believes that motherhood is a high calling with the responsibility of shaping and molding the children who will one day define who we are as a community and a nation.
4. The Proverbs 31 woman is a disciplined and industrious keeper of the home who creates a warm and loving environment for her family and friends.
5. The Proverbs 31 woman contributes to the financial well-being of her household by being a faithful steward of the time and money God has entrusted to her.
6. The Proverbs 31 woman speaks with wisdom and faithful instruction as she mentors and supports other women, and develops godly friendships.
7. The Proverbs 31 woman shares the love of Christ by extending her hands to help with the needs in the community.

Ministries Features

Magazine: *P31 Woman* is our monthly publication packed with information and encouragement to equip and inspire women in the **Seven Principles** of the Proverbs 31 woman.

Radio Ministry: The 2-minute Proverbs 31 radio program currently airs on approximately 200 networks around the world.

Speaking Ministry: Proverbs 31 Ministries believes in the value of women encouraging other women. Our ministry to speakers and writers exists to train and equip women to do just this. We hold an annual **Speakers'/Writers' Training Conference** each summer and are taking registrations online. If you are interested in having one of our speakers come to your church, convention, or special event, please contact us at the information below.

On-line Community Ministry: Proverbs 31 Ministries offers an Online community Ministry. The purpose of the Online Community Ministry is to provide a place of encouragement and support for women who want to be **"the woman of noble character"** as described in **Proverbs 31:10–31.**

For a sample issue of our magazine, or more information on the ministries, write or call:

Proverbs 31 Ministries
616-G Matthews-Mint Hill Road
Matthews, NC 28105
877-p31-home (877-731-4663)
web site: www.proverbs31.org

In order to experience the ultimate makeover, we must begin with the ultimate truth.

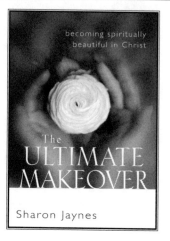

ISBN: 0-8024-3556-4

Women desire to be beautiful. However, many fail to realize that beauty begins on the inside and works its way out. But how do you become beautiful from the inside? You will not discover the secret in magazines, on talk shows, or in secular self-help books. Becoming beautiful from the inside out is a feat only God can do.

Come join Sharon Jaynes and discover an inner beauty treatment with lasting results with the makeover artist Himself—Jesus Christ.

Whether you're a brand new believer or a seasoned saint, this step-by-step guide to becoming spiritually beautiful is a perfect fit. Sharon's writing style is neither stuffy nor fluffy as she gently sloughs away our misconceptions about what it means to be a follower of Christ.
　　Liz Curtis Higgs, Best-selling author of *Bad Girls of the Bible*

MOODY
PUBLISHERS
THE NAME YOU CAN TRUST.

1-800-678-6928 www.MoodyPublishers.org

S INCE 1894, Moody Publishers has been dedicated to equip and motivate people to advance the cause of Christ by publishing evangelical Christian literature and other media for all ages, around the world. Because we are a ministry of the Moody Bible Institute of Chicago, a portion of the proceeds from the sale of this book go to train the next generation of Christian leaders.

If we may serve you in any way in your spiritual journey toward understanding Christ and the Christian life, please contact us at www.moodypublishers.com.

"All Scripture is God-breathed and is useful for teaching, rebuking, correcting and training in righteousness, so that the man of God may be thoroughly equipped for every good work."
—*2 TIMOTHY 3:16, 17*

MOODY
PUBLISHERS
THE NAME YOU CAN TRUST®

BEING A GREAT MOM, RAISING GREAT KIDS TEAM

ACQUIRING EDITOR
Elsa Mazon

COVER DESIGN
Ragont Design

INTERIOR DESIGN
Ragont Design

PRINTING AND BINDING
Versa Press, Inc.